Improving library and information services through self-assessment

A guide for senior managers
and staff developers

Improving library and information services through self-assessment

A guide for senior managers and staff developers

British Library Research and Innovation Report 172

Margaret Kinnell
Dean of Faculty of Science, Loughborough University

Bob Usherwood
Professor in Librarianship, Department of Information Studies, University of Sheffield

Kathryn Jones
Contract Researcher

LIBRARY ASSOCIATION PUBLISHING
LONDON

The opinions expressed in this report are those of the authors and not necessarily those of the British Library.

Published by
Library Association Publishing
7 Ridgmount Street
London WC1E 7AE

Library Association Publishing is wholly owned by The Library Association.

Published 1999

British Library Cataloguing in Publication Data
A catalogue record for this book is available from the British Library.

RIC/G/345
ISSN 1366-8218
ISBN 1-85604-336-3

Typeset in 11/14pt Bergamo and Franklin Gothic Condensed from author's disk by Library Association Publishing.
Printed and made in Great Britain by MPG Books Ltd, Bodmin, Cornwall.

Contents

1
Introducing self-assessment

Introduction

An increasing number of public and private sector organizations are using self-assessment as a means of regularly and systematically assessing their achievements against a model of good management practice, as part of their drive to continuously improve their services or products. Crucially, the process of self-assessment focuses on achievement rather than audit, and unlike other quality tools it is designed for long-term rather than short-term use. Sustaining continuous improvement is the aim (TQMI, 1995). The results of the assessments are then used to identify current strengths and weaknesses, and to plan the actions required for future improvement. The principle of an organization regularly checking its performance against best practice is also well established within the context of self-assessment (Conti, 1997).

How can the self-assessment techniques described in this book support library managers in developing the quality of their services? Our aim is to provide a simple, effective and tested method for improving library services' planning of quality services and for reviewing service delivery. This book and the accompanying training pack (*The library and information services self-assessment training pack*, separately available from Library Association Publishing, see page 3), offer comprehensive guidelines for undertaking self-assessment in library and information services. The training pack provides the necessary documentation to deliver a training programme which covers the principles and techniques of self-assessment and post-assessment planning. Our aim is to provide a thorough examination of the concept and principles of self-assessment within the public information and library sector, together with the means to implement it.

This chapter consists of two sections. First, the contents, aims and objectives of the book and training pack are described. Guidance on how the book and training pack can be used by public information and library sector managers is also provided. The second section, on the origins of quality management in the public sector, contains a brief summary of the research project 'Assessment tools for quality management in public libraries' (funded by the British Library) to offer a context and background to the development of the training pack.

The material provided

This section summarizes the contents of this book and the training pack, *The library and information services self-assessment training pack*. Full guidance on who should be using the material and how it should be used or tailored is also given.

The book

The aim of the book is to offer detailed and comprehensive guidelines for library and information managers considering implementing self-assessment programmes within their services. The book is aimed at library and information professionals who have some understanding of the management approaches already being undertaken within library services.

The first three chapters of the book provide the necessary background to self-assessment in the public information and library sector. Chapter 2 details the growth of quality management and self-assessment in the public information and library sector. It establishes the context of the public information and library sector: government departments, public libraries, academic libraries and local government information services. It explores the theoretical, social, cultural and political context of quality management and self-assessment in the public information and library sector. It examines the current pressures on managers across public information and library services, detailing the reasons why there is now a demand for the accurate assessment of service achievements.

Chapter 3 critiques the current application of quality management in the public information and library sector. It identifies a number of reasons why organizations should undertake self-assessment, and examines the value and impact that self-assessment can make on library and information service management.

Chapter 4 outlines the criteria and model against which library and information services will be self-assessed. It identifies the core values of the model and shows how these relate to library and information services.

Chapter 5 provides guidelines for managers seeking to undertake self-assessment in their organization. It identifies the relevant issues which should be addressed, such as the support of senior managers, the choice of approach, and whether or how to tailor and adapt the approach. Drawing on the experiences of the demonstrator services and on the literature, it explores and examines the process in order to identify critical success factors for implementing self-assessment within a library and information service, across all sectors.

Chapter 6 deals with the issue of how quality management and self-assessment initiatives might be maintained. This chapter includes a discussion of how self-assessment can inform the planning process, and how benchmarking can improve library and information services.

Finally, Chapter 7 makes recommendations on the development of self-assessment criteria for library and information services. It also makes recommendations for the implementation and promotion of self-assessment within the library and information sector.

The library and information services self-assessment training pack

This training pack and toolkit contains all the necessary documents for developing a training programme and undertaking a self-assessment within a public information and library service. It is separately available from Library Association Publishing, 7 Ridgmount Street, London WC1E 7AE (Tel: 020 7636 7543; from October 1999 020 7255 0594).

THE TRAINING PACK

The training pack aims to provide a simple and effective approach to understanding and implementing self-assessment. It has been designed for use in groups of no more than 12 people. The materials accompanying the guidelines can be photocopied and used in multiple sessions.

The training pack contains two sections:

- Section 1 provides an introduction to the pack and offers guidelines for the development of training programmes.
- Section 2 outlines six training sessions. These provide a structured approach to introducing the concepts and techniques of self-assessment to library services. Each session outline provides guidance for trainers on key learning points, content and overall objectives. Relevant overhead transparencies, session handouts and exercises are also provided.

THE TOOLKIT

The toolkit contains documentation for undertaking a comprehensive self-assessment in library and information services. These tools have been developed in the specific context of the public information and library sector. Four sections of the resource pack comprise the toolkit:

- Section 3 contains the library and information sector improvement model (LISIM) - the model of good practice the unit will be assessed against.
- Section 4 contains the self-assessment criteria which were derived from LISIM. These criteria offer explicit guidelines on the issues which should be considered in the assessment.
- Section 5 contains the self-assessment pro-forma, the tool for undertaking self-assessment.
- Section 6 contains the self-assessment scoring workbook, for those library services which decide to score their assessment.

How to use the materials

The book and resource pack have been developed in order to facilitate the development of self-assessment programmes within library and information units. However, the material has been designed so it can be tailored to specific organizations' requirements. The pack can be used as a whole training course to be completed over two days, or as short course material to be used in one- or two-hour sessions. The pack contains a complete training course covering the whole self-assessment process from initial discussions on its potential value to the implementation of the toolkit and the post-assessment planning phase.

TAILORING THE CONTENTS TO LIBRARY SERVICES

The training pack has been developed to ensure flexibility in approach and application. There are opportunities to tailor each session to suit the requirements of individual library services. Guidance on these considerations are given in Chapter 5.

Who should use the materials

The material has been developed to be used across library and information services by the users listed in Table 1.1.

Table 1.1 *Appropriate users*

Materials	Appropriate users
The book	Senior managers
	Lead assessment manager
	Assessment team
	Library staff
The training pack and toolkit	Lead assessment manager
	Assessment team

The origins of quality management in the public sector

The 1990s have seen a sea change in the management of public sector services. There has been increasing pressure on these organizations not only to demonstrate their value for money, but also to prove their worth. External inspections and audits, for example by the Audit Commission, have become an increasing factor in public sector management. The pressure to demonstrate value for money, to meet users' expectations, and to attain higher standards, has given rise to the need to supply appropriate evidence that efficient and effective management practices are in place, to local citizens and local and national fund-holders.

These pressures originated in various central government initiatives such as compulsory competitive tendering, the Citizen's Charter, and now Best Value. Public sector organizations can no longer assume that they are immune by virtue of serving the public good. They have to offer concrete evidence of their efficient and effective management. At the same time there is an increasing demand to improve public sector management practices through the principles of economy, efficiency and effectiveness. This new public sector management ethos borrowed many of the management techniques being applied across the private sector, including the concepts captured in the term 'total quality management' (TQM). Consequently a number of public sector organizations have embraced many of the principles of TQM.

Many local authorities, government agencies and the National Health Service were among those public sector services to adopt 'total quality' as a cornerstone of their management principles and practices. Higher education institutions and schools were also faced with the need to develop quality management as a consequence of more stringent assessment procedures. These organizations were seeking to improve services and match them to user requirements. Various initiatives and approaches were adopted in the push for quality, such as standards, specifications and service-level agreements. However, despite the rhetoric of improved services, the assessment of organizational achievement tended to be subjective. Indeed, these techniques lent themselves to ensuring conformance to requirements rather than to ensuring continuous improvement in the management and achievements of the organization. Unless the organization was prepared to apply for awards and accolades, such as the Charter Mark or ISO 9000, the evaluation of quality initiatives had no external validation. There was therefore a need for a rigorous, objective assessment of quality which could be validated externally as well as internally.

The development of self-assessment models in the public and private sectors

At the same time that various total quality techniques were being adopted by the public and private sectors, there was a move to create national standards for quality management. Some of these standards took the form of awards which, it was hoped, would not only serve as a framework for organizations implementing total quality, but increase the adoption of the practices of good management across private sector organizations. The implementation of awards such as The Malcolm Baldrige National Quality Award or the European Quality Award by various European multinational companies was in part an attempt to increase the competitiveness of this sector in the face of competition from the Far East (Easton, 1995). These awards provided a context for organizations to understand what was involved in adopting total quality principles, and offered a framework for the self-assessment of achievements. Indeed, American research has shown that 'many more companies use the Baldrige award criteria for diagnostic purposes than apply or ever intend to apply for the award' (Easton, 1995, 14).

Quality awards were developed to reflect the principles and ideals of good management practice identified by quality management 'gurus' such as Juran, Feigenbaum, Crosby and Deming. The awards provided a model of good practice, and established criteria for achieving excellence in the key areas of leadership, employee management, process management, development of policy and strategy, and management of relationships with customers and other stakeholders. The criteria generally ask organizations to consider basic questions such as:

- What are we doing?
- Why are we doing it?
- How will we get there?
- How will we know when we get there?

The process of answering these questions enables organizations to discover what they have achieved in relation to what they set out to achieve, as well as to identify the difference between 'perception' and 'fact' in relation to their results – in other words, the difference between what they *think* they have achieved and what they *know* they have achieved.

While these awards were originally developed for the private sector, there was soon a move to adopt the criteria and apply them to the public sector. For example, the European Foundation for Quality Management (EFQM, 1997) published public sector guidelines a few months after the private sector award was inaugurated. However, it was not until 1995 that public sector organizations were able to apply for the European Quality Award. Within the UK, the Henderson Report proposed that the British Quality Award should follow the guidelines established by the EFQM (Henderson, 1992). By 1995, guidelines for British public sector organizations were published, with special reference to the health sector, local government and the uniformed services. Following research undertaken by the Cabinet Office in 1996, specific guidelines were also created for central government agencies.

As a result of these activities there is now a growing number of UK public and private sector organizations such as the Benefits Agency, the Post Office and the Inland Revenue who are using self-assessment techniques in order to determine and demonstrate their success in achieving total quality. However, the low level of take-up by library and information services of self-assessment, identified in British Library research into both public library services and academic libraries (Brockman, 1997), suggested the need for an approach specifically tuned to managing the public and not-for-profit information and library sector within the new management context.

Background to the development of the toolkit

The research indicated that although senior managers acknowledged the importance of quality management initiatives, they were generally critical of those models and techniques which had not been developed specifically for the public sector. The research also showed that many private sector organizations were considering self assessment as a powerful diagnostic and planning tool, and concluded that assessment against an externally validated quality management model might be one way of addressing current pressures on the public information and library sector:

> Research testing appropriate methods and models should be undertaken to support public libraries in their adoption of quality management. This should include investigations of the potential offered by self-assessment and of the democratic approach to quality in the public sector. (Milner, Kinnell and Usherwood, 1997, 221)

Prior to the development of the public information and library sector toolkit, work undertaken by the Office of Public Services and the British Quality Foundation suggested that self-assessment has the potential to become a useful management tool for the public sector. However, there had been no formal work to determine the relevance of self-diagnosis techniques for library and information units. Therefore in 1996 the British Library Research and Innovation Centre funded a two-year study to examine the potential of self-assessment for public library services. While the work was developed to meet public library needs, the principles and practices of self-assessment are clearly relevant to all library and information services, including, for example, those in the higher education sector.

Three approaches were investigated and recommendations for their implementation made. The three quality management approaches which were investigated are described in more detail below. There are slight differences in their emphasis, but they share several characteristics:

- They are all applicable to the public sector. Two (The Democratic Approach and The Quality Framework) were developed specifically with the public sector in mind, the third (The Business Excellence Model) was adapted from a model created for the private sector.
- They each stress the importance of tackling human resource needs and customer satisfaction, both key issues for public libraries.
- They enable library services to integrate any quality programmes already in place. Initiatives such as customer satisfaction surveys, Charter Mark, Investors in People (IiP), quality standards and specifications could be tied in with these models.

THE MODELS

Of the three self-assessment approaches to quality management that were selected for consideration in this study, the Business Excellence Model (Figure 1.1) was highlighted at an early stage because it offered perhaps the most structured approach. As noted above, it had also been widely used in the private sector and specifically adapted for the public sector. The model clearly outlined nine assessment criteria and provided 32 sub-criteria.

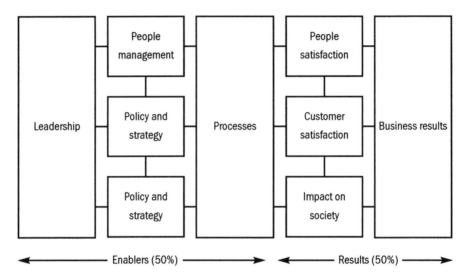

Fig. 1.1 *The European Quality Foundation Business Excellence Model (EFQM 1997)*

The Quality Framework (Figure 1.2) offered a foundation for those who wanted to consider how to develop quality management in the public sector. Stewart and Walsh (1989) argued that public services operate within a context which requires special consideration. The quality of the surroundings and the service relationship would influence customer perception and satisfaction as much as the service which was received. Therefore, it is argued, any quality management model must take this into account.

Pfeffer and Coote's Democratic Approach (1991) offered an understanding of quality management within the modern welfare state (Figure 1.3). They argued that, although existing approaches to quality manage-

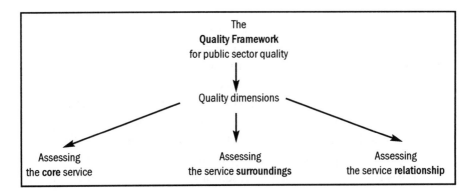

Fig. 1.2   *The Quality Framework (Stewart and Walsh, 1989)*

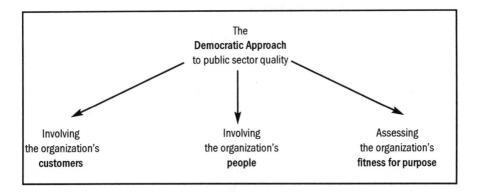

Fig. 1.3   *The Democratic Approach to quality (Pfeffer and Coote, 1991)*

ment have much to offer, they failed to take account of key ideological differences between the public and private sectors. The main difference is that the public sector is charged with serving the interest of the community as a whole and in meeting the needs of individuals within the community.

While the Quality Framework and the Democratic Approach had not provided explicit self-assessment criteria, it was considered that the approaches outlined would lend themselves to self-assessment techniques. The aim was to offer a self-assessment toolkit for public library services which took account of their requirements within the local government structure and also the complex stakeholder relationships that needed to be managed. It is this dimension in particular which is so relevant to other sectors. Managing a range of relationships – with suppliers, funders, clients, user communities and others – is a key issue for all library and information services. Any quality management tools and techniques to support continuous improvement have to consider stakeholder relationships and the operating environment as being crucially important.

As the project developed it also became clear that the self-assessment concept could be extended to meet the needs of library and information services in other public sector organizations, and the self-assessment toolkit was therefore discussed with senior colleagues in the academic and health sectors.

Methodological framework

While the overarching methodological framework was the use of three demonstrator services (the most that could be accommodated given the complexity of the issues and the depth of analysis required), these were underpinned by the use of action research techniques. Action research ensured the reliability and validity of the outcomes of the research process, ie the self-assessment toolkit and training materials. An inherent principle of the methodological framework was that the actions of the practitioners were critical to the successful completion of the project. The research process was designed to ensure that these practitioners were able to own and collaborate on the research project. Not only were the demonstrator services the focus of the research, they were also asked to manage the project elements within their own organization.

The choice of demonstrator services was influenced by the requirement to test self-assessment within different local government contexts, ie a London borough, a metropolitan county and a shire county. Care was also taken to ensure that these authorities reflected a variety of approaches to quality management in terms of applying quality processes and their level of maturity in implementing quality.

Comparative case studies are an increasingly common research technique within the social policy and public management sector. They are generally considered to be more robust and methodologically sound than single case studies, because evidence to support theoretical suppositions is drawn from a number of sources. In this case the evidence to support the theoretical and analytical inferences was drawn from documents, interviews and observation. Given the need to produce toolkits for local application, it was also essential to ensure that the research strategy was flexible enough to introduce changes without impacting on the ultimate reliability and validity of the results. In effect, a first-level replication of the research strategy was adopted. At the beginning of each research phase the same research instrument was used in each of the services. However, as and when feedback was given to the research team, the research instruments were modified to fit local contexts. The research team met with the demonstrator services at each phase of the project to support managers in developing and testing the models.

International contacts were established with German and Swedish library authorities, using the good offices of the Deutsches Bibliotheksinstitut and the network established by the research team (see Borchardt in References). These took longer to establish than had been foreseen, and so replication of the UK methodology was not possible. However, there was opportunity to test some of the self-assessment tools and the draft self-assessment toolkit to identify the potential of the toolkit for wider international contexts. This was seen to be a useful means of testing its robustness. The results were encouraging, and input from a wider range of European public library services was achieved through a seminar during the 1998 IFLA Conference in Amsterdam.

Two project seminar/workshops were held - the first in February 1998 and the second at the end of the project in January 1999. These included representation by the demonstrator services and invited participants working at senior levels in the public information and library sector, public sector and quality organizations (eg British Quality Foundation, European Foundation for Quality Management, Cabinet Office, Health and Safety Executive). Further data were gathered using discussion groups in the workshops as well as disseminating project findings to senior managers.

Links with other relevant British Library projects were also developed, to ensure data sharing. These included the Social Audit of Public Libraries (Usherwood and Linley, Sheffield University) and Investors in People in Library and Information Services (Goulding, et al, Loughborough University). Networking with the British Quality Foundation Public Sector Group was also undertaken, and a seminar was hosted by the project team at Loughborough University to disseminate the public library model to other public sector managers in order to gain further feedback.

Research phases

The project was split into two phases. In the first phase a member of the research team gained accreditation in self-assessment techniques and the concepts of self assessment were introduced to the demonstrator services. A quality audit was undertaken in each of the organizations. The aim was to understand how quality initiatives were perceived and understood within the context of the information and library service. Semi-structured interviews were carried out with between six and eight people in each authority, and relevant documentation was collected and analysed (policy documentation, etc). The emphasis was on auditing the planning, communication, review and assessment of quality initiatives within the organization. Issues relating to customer focus, the management of people, stakeholder involvement, and the planning and evaluation of service initiatives were discussed in feedback sessions. The first project seminar/workshop was then held.

In phase two the research team worked with the demonstrator services to identify which quality model or models they wished to develop and implement in their organization. The core values of the three approaches were introduced to the authorities, and they were asked to identify those values they considered to be a priority for their organization. These core values were: customer focus; equity in service; an open system; public participation; visible and visionary leadership; employee development; involvement and satisfaction; continuous improvement; management by fact; partnership development; consistency of purpose; process management; public responsibility, and stakeholder consideration. The analysis of the core values is discussed in more detail by Jones, Kinnell and Usherwood (1999).

A gap analysis of the 'fit' of the demonstrator services against the models was then undertaken, which then formed the basis of the self-assessment model that was selected as most appropriate to all the services. Only two of the services were able to complete this stage effectively during the period of the project. One service encountered organizational difficulties due to restructuring and elected to undertake the work at a later date. The two services then undertook self assessment using tools developed for them, and trialled the Library and Information Sector Improvement Model (LISIM) that formed the basis for the toolkit and training pack. These were also tested on the demonstrator services and, as indicated above, were also discussed more widely within the library and information sector. These comments, and feedback from the wider library and information profession supported the creation of the toolkit and training pack. The discussions throughout this book are illustrated where relevant by the demonstrator services' experiences and also with reference to the literature on the subject. The second project seminar/workshop was then held, and finally the report, book and toolkit were completed.

Conclusions

Self-assessment can offer managers a focused and systematic evaluation of the way in which they manage their services. As a management technique, it is being increasingly adopted across public sector services. While research has shown that the concept of self-assessment is applicable to the public sector, many library and information managers remain sceptical of its value. The 'self-assessment tools' project investigated the potential of self-assessment for the information and library sector, and showed that the process does have a real and valid potential. However, to ensure its efficient and effective use, the approach must be adapted and tailored to specific service contexts.

References

Borchardt, P (1999) Qualitätsmanagement in der Bibliothek umsetzen - wie geht das? Ergebnisse eines britischen Projekts, *Buch und Bibliothek*, **51**, 60-1.

Brockman, J (ed) (1997) *Quality management and benchmarking in the information sector*, Bowker-Saur.

Conti, T (1997) *Organisational self-assessment*, Chapman & Hall.

Easton, G (1995) A Baldrige examiner's assessment of US total quality management. In Cole, R E (ed) *The death and life of the American quality movement*, Oxford University Press.

EFQM (1997) *Guide to self-assessment 1997*, European Foundation for Quality Management.

Henderson, D (1992) *Report on the feasibility of a new UK quality award*, Department of Trade and Industry.

Jones, K, Kinnell, M and Usherwood, B (1999) *Planning for public library improvement: report of the second project workshop*, Department of Information and Library Studies, Loughborough University.

Milner, E, Kinnell, M and Usherwood, B (1997) Quality management and public library services. In Brockman, J (ed) *Quality management and benchmarking in the information sector*, Bowker-Saur.

Pfeffer, N and Coote, A (1991) *Is quality good for you?*, Institute of Public Policy Research.

Stewart, J and Walsh, K (1989) *The search for quality*, Local Government Training Board.

TQMI (1995) *What is self-assessment?*, TQM International.

2

Quality in context

Introduction

In recent decades, public sector management literature has been dominated by the need to improve the efficiency and effectiveness of working practices, and as a consequence the service that is delivered to the end-user. Many of the concepts, theories and models which have been offered as _possible solutions have been suggested under the umbrella of Total Quality Management, eg ISO 9000, standards and specifications. These principles have been welcomed by many as offering a potential lifeline to the public sector, which has been operating within the context of stringent budget cuts and other pressures such as external audits and inspections. In particular, those techniques with an inherent focus on meeting customer needs and which concentrate on the development of human resources have become increasingly popular within the public sector, such as Charter Mark and Investors in People. However, a dichotomy seems to be emerging between the rhetoric and the reality of the adoption of quality techniques within the public sector, and in particular the public information and library sector (Usherwood, 1996).

Despite the fact that quality forms a substantial part of the library-management literature, the problems and issues which face library and information managers implementing quality management have not dissipated. Where there has appeared to be a swift and widespread uptake in quality techniques, evidence suggests that there has in fact been a relatively low level of formal approaches adopted (Milner, Kinnell and Usherwood, 1997). An inherent problem appears to be the uncritical use of management techniques originally developed in the private sector (Kerslake and Kinnell, 1996).

Many articles advocating the quality management approach do little more than address the practicalities of implementing the various methods these schemes entail. There has been little reported critique or criticism of these methods within the profession (Brockman, 1997). Those that do advocate caution when implementing quality management (Usherwood, 1992) are often accused of missing the point (Clayton, 1993). Outside the information sector, however, there has been a growing debate on the impact, importance and credibility of quality management within the public sector (Wilkinson and Willmott, 1995; Kirkpatrick and Martinez Lucio, 1995).

Although quality management no longer appears to be considered 'just another management fad' as a management tool, it has yet to gain real acceptance across the library and information profession. In part, these difficulties have arisen because there has been no serious attempt to define an appropriate model or approach to quality management for the public library and information sector. The 'Self-assessment tools' project has endeavoured to address this problem and to offer potential solutions for the implementation of appropriate and acceptable routes to achieving best practice.

This chapter shows how changing management practices led to the widespread adoption of quality management techniques across the public information sector. It examines the growth and development of these management approaches. The aim is not to provide an analysis of different tools and techniques, rather it is to highlight those critical issues which still need addressing when considering the use and development of quality programmes within the library and information sector.

The context of quality management in the public sector

The 1980s and 1990s saw a radical shift in the management practices employed in the public sector. This transformation manifested itself in the introduction of new management mechanisms designed to increase the effectiveness of public sector services; through, for example, compulsory competitive tendering in local government, the Financial Management Initiative in the Civil Service and the introduction of the internal market in the National Health Service. Indeed, the watchwords of these new management techniques were economy, efficiency and effectiveness. These changes have not taken place without a great deal of debate as to their value or appropriateness. The Labour Government has now pledged to remove the internal market in the National Health Service.

In particular there was concern that the push to improving quality was aligned too closely with the pressure to reduce costs and expenditure in the public sector (Wilkinson and Willmott, 1995), and, as Freeman-Bell and Grover (1994, 567) argued, those advocating these new techniques did not allow for the extra resources that might be required:

> The government is taking the view that measures such as the Citizens' Charter and benchmarking can be introduced without additional cost. In our view this is unrealistic . . . this attitude ignores the front-end loading of the costs of introducing new systems.

Defining quality within the public information sector

Even with the rhetoric of quality improvement in the public sector, there seems to be little agreement on what 'quality' actually means (Kinnell, 1995; Davies and Kirkpatrick, 1995). There have been attempts to define quality in the context of the public sector (eg Morgan and Murgatroyd, 1994), but the concepts and ideologies of the private sector still prevail. Total quality management, quality assurance, business restructuring and quality control, are all terms which appear in the professional journals, and bring with them definitions and rules from the perspective of the private sector. However, it has been argued that, while the new 'managerialism' strengthened the claims to proficiency in public sector management, the uncritical adoption of techniques based on private sector principles did not allow for the true nature of public sector services to come to light:

> The mistake is to assume that there is one approach to management applicable to public services based on an over-simplified model of the private sector . . . the use of quasi-markets and a stress on private sector values creates

> problems if the limits to their application in the public domain are not
> recognised. (Stewart and Walsh, 1992, 518).

Few have attempted to translate these new management initiatives into
public sector terminology, let alone modify them according to the stand-
point of the library and information profession. Instead they have allowed
the rhetoric of the private sector to invade the culture and mind-set of
public service management; yet, as Pfeffer and Coote (1991, 31) warn,
'once quality leaves the commercial world, rules and relationships change
and it loses its clarity of purpose'.

It has been suggested that there is a real need for an adequate definition
of quality management in the context of the public information and
library sector, in order to counter

> the strong body of feeling which suggests, occasionally forcefully, that man-
> agement philosophies and techniques associated with the commercial sec-
> tor are not always appropriate for use in public libraries. (Milner, Kinnell
> and Usherwood, 1997, 213)

In particular there seems to be a tension surrounding the use of the management concepts of economy, efficiency and effectiveness as the basis for
public sector definitions of quality management. While these ideas are
accepted as critical to service provision (Carter et al, 1992), many have
argued that the notion of *equity* must also be accounted for in definitions
of quality in public sector services (Maxwell, 1984; Carter et al, 1992).
Equity ensures that all citizens receive public services appropriate to their
needs, and emphasizes the need for appropriate choice (Pfeffer and Coote,
1991).

Indeed, it has been argued that the need to ensure equity or fairness in
service distribution is what distinguishes public sector organizations from
the commercial sector. The difficulty is, however, that in order to provide
appropriate services to every individual, economies of scale are reduced,
so equity may in fact require extra resources, something which resource
providers might be less likely to accept.

A related issue is the problem of defining the users of public sector services. There has been much criticism about the use of the term 'customer'
in this context. Many feel that relationships within the public sector are

far more complex than this concept acknowledges. For example, who are the 'customers' of public libraries? Are they the people who borrow the books, or the society that benefits from the education of its members? Is it right to identify users of libraries as customers? It has been claimed that using the term 'customer' to describe library users 'undervalues the role of library membership as an active form of citizenship, education and personal self-development' (Burton et al, 1996, 66). What about 'stake-holders'? Are these terms that library services do, or should, subscribe to? The complexity of stakeholder relationships within the public sector, and in particular the notion of indirect stakeholders – eg the society that benefits from the education of its members – requires attention in those models of good management practice that are tailored or adapted for the public sector.

Many have argued that within the public library and information sector the concept of quality is also distinguishable through its inseparability from the service that is received by the end-user (Milner, Kinnell and Usherwood, 1997). That is, the interaction between the user and the service provider has an important impact on the quality of service received: Wilding (1994, 59) suggests that 'the quality of these relationships is crucial to the quality of the service'. Indeed, in many instances this customer-service interaction will be the 'product' that the library service is providing, such as enquiry work. This intangibility holds within it a distinctiveness that must be accounted for in definitions of library and information quality management, but that is often missing in private sector models. As Brockman (1997, 5) argues, 'quality becomes a meaningful concept only when it is indissolubly linked to the aim of total customer satisfaction'.

Research has shown that practitioners within the library and information field have developed their own understanding of quality. In particular, most definitions seem to relate to performance measurement or to more formal approaches to achieving quality such as the former BS 5750 (Garrod and Kinnell, 1997).

There is a growing argument, however, that what matters is not how individual organizations define quality, but how they actually implement it. As the Audit Commission report *Putting quality on the map* (1993, 3) suggests, 'whatever definition or concept of quality is used, the vital point is how to put it into practice'.

Yet without a commonly defined approach or understanding of what is meant by quality within the public sector, there is a real danger that it will be too readily dismissed, especially by those who are sceptical of the new management attitudes and techniques which are now being introduced. Porter (1992, 240) argues that unless these types of question are answered and the nature and validity of different approaches to quality examined, there is every chance that

> at best we may be misled into introducing models appropriate to needs. At worst we may reject the whole idea of quality because we cannot find a consensus.

The lack of common definition also presents practical problems once the initiatives have been implemented. Those organizations wishing to benchmark their practices, for example, will not have a common frame of reference within which to work.

A holistic view of what quality management is within the library and information profession that takes account of these perspectives has been described as follows:

> Quality management is both an underpinning philosophy and a variety of tools and techniques, which focus the organisational structure, its resources, the people within it and the views of all relevant stakeholders on attaining and continuously improving measurable organisational objectives informed by the preferences and needs of the end-user. (Milner, Kinnell and Usherwood, 1997, 213)

The customer of the public sector

The requirement to make public services more accountable and responsive to the *sovereign citizen* has been the underlying philosophy behind many of the new management practices adopted within the public sector. Citizens were no longer thought of as the 'users' or 'recipients' of public services, but as their 'purchasers' or 'clients'. Using the language of the market was intended to create an element of choice in the public sector. Citizens were to be empowered to make decisions about the type of services they wished to receive. The public sector was to be more responsive to the needs of their consumers; for example, local authorities had to take account of the opinions of local residents when making service-level decisions.

As the discussion in the previous section has shown, however, a key criticism of the approaches to quality defined in the private sector is that public sector organizations serve more than one type of customer: the customer as an individual and the customer as society. There was also a lack of acknowledgement that public services can have more complex relationships with their customers or users. At a basic level, commercial-sector customers have the right to exit any relationship by taking their business elsewhere. In the public sector, however, the service on offer may be the only option available to the customer.

To counteract these difficulties, many approaches to quality have attempted to include some form of customer-service standards. This process has been readily embodied in the Citizen's Charter, where the rights of customers are outlined in terms of the services they can expect and what they can do if they do not receive them (Walsh, 1995). However, these 'procedural rights' (Pfeffer and Coote, 1991) are not without difficulties, such as how the service can specify in sufficient detail what the user is entitled to (Walsh, 1995). Again, there has been criticism levelled at the implementation of these new management techniques simply because it does not take into account the additional effort required in such an undertaking:

> rights-based approaches to quality require complex and extensive organisation and administrative back-up (Wilding, 1994, 69).

Within the public library and information sector there is an added difficulty presented by the notion of customer accountability. The 'rights-based' approach has the benefit of increasing users' expectations of the types of services they are entitled to and should receive. However, in the information sector there has been a long history of increasing levels of customer satisfaction juxtaposed with concern among practitioners about depleted book-stocks and the closure of branches (Aslib, 1995). Here, it appears that customers either do not hold high expectations of what the library service should be delivering or would prefer any service to none at all. Therefore there is a real need to educate customers and other stake-holders on what the library service can achieve and thus to raise their expectations. Appropriate levels of library and information service provision must be defined and assessed with adequate rigour, in order to ensure that stakeholders are made aware of disparities in service provision.

Another issue related to customer participation in decision-making is who should be involved in the process. Should non-users have as large a role to play as frequent users? What about new users compared with long-standing users? Which age-groups should be accounted for in the decision-making process - at what level should children be allowed to determine what they want? Many libraries have implemented some form of customer comments scheme, but there also need to be opportunities to participate in different types of decision-making, eg stock selection, service levels, opening hours. There is also the question of how much influence customers should be allowed. Mechanisms need to be put into place to inform and educate citizens on how they can influence decisions. Again, this may require additional resources which frequently do not seem to be accounted for, as McKevitt and Lawton (1996, 51) suggests:

> that customer charters . . . may raise customer or client expectations is an additional burden on middle managers and front-line staff who may not be allocated resources for training or increased investment in facilities.

Performance assessment in the public sector

> As we move into a more commercial and competitive environment, management's needs are likely to change. Not only will we need to monitor services to maintain quality and quantity, but we are likely to need to ensure that we know what we are recording and what targets we are setting. (Pybus, quoted in Milner, Kinnell and Usherwood, 1997, 131)

The need for adequate performance measurement has been inherent in many of the new initiatives adopted in public sector organizations, such as the Charter Mark. However, there are a number of issues which need to be addressed within this context, principally who should be involved in the assessment and what form it should take. There is a real need to consider 'whose quality is it anyway?' - on whose judgement should decisions regarding success or failure be based? The move to customer and stakeholder accountability in the public sector suggests that all stakeholders (politicians, funding councils, senior managers, staff, suppliers, customers) should be involved in the assessment process. However, if this is true then there is a need to decide what individual stakeholders can assess. Stewart and Walsh's approach to quality would suggest that, while non-experts can readily assess the service surroundings and service relationships, their assessment of the core service may not reflect an accurate picture of what is achieved (Freeman-Bell and Grover, 1994). Library users may, for example, be able to judge the attitude of library staff, but they may not necessarily be able to assess how efficiently their query was answered. They may be able to gauge the usefulness of the material provided, but will not be able to judge the proficiency with which it was obtained. In effect, what is required is a varied approach which enables different assessment measures and indicators to be used in the evaluation of services, as McKevitt and Lawton (1996, 54) argue:

> in recognising that public sector organisations are influenced by a multiplicity of stakeholders, it may then be unrealistic to expect any system of performance measurement to satisfy the interests of all stakeholders.

However, there are also issues to bear in mind when considering what service achievements can be assessed in the public sector. The impact of public sector activities on the wider society, is rarely addressed in performance measures, eg how libraries can influence educational attainment levels, as Henty suggests (1989, 77):

> The theory that institutions have definable outcomes which can be readily measured has gained increasing credibility and has put pressure on institutions in the educational and cultural spheres to state their objectives and develop techniques to measure them. In the library context, this has led to a situation in which library services are being seen in terms of measurable activity rather than a generalised public good.

Some innovative work on the value and impact of public library services has been undertaken recently. Usherwood and Linley at the University of

Sheffield (1998) developed a 'Social Process Audit' of public library services. They showed that qualitative data could provide substantial and valid evidence of the social impact of library services. This type of data could be used to reinforce and corroborate the dry statistical measures often used in service-level decision-making.

In order to make this process as rigorous as possible, an assessment would also need to consider performance against best-in-class organizations. This notion is inherent in new initiatives such as Best Value.

Other issues

A member of the EFQM suggested recently that self-assessment requires a long-term commitment of at least five years (Jones, Kinnell and Usherwood, 1999). Yet today's library managers are under increasing pressure to provide quick returns on investment.

There is a desire among those working in the public sector to develop methods and techniques for quality management which take account of their organizational structure and acknowledge the significance of the culture of their parent organization. Between them, the demonstrator services faced local government reorganization, budget cuts and restructuring during the course of the research. In such a climate quality often becomes at best sidelined, at worst ignored. As responsibilities for the service's development change, it is difficult to maintain any impetus in quality programmes.

At times of change, quality management programmes are often put on hold. It is hard to motivate staff to achieve quality if they are in fear of their jobs. Equally, in times of budget cuts, quality programmes are often viewed with scepticism by staff who know what could really be achieved if enough funds were available. However, part of this problem lies with how people in organizations view quality. The original impetus to achieve quality can affect how people perceive it. If, as is the case in many public sector organizations, quality management was introduced by senior managers at the behest of local politicians, there is a danger that it may be seen as an unnecessary burden.

The public library and information sector

Library and information services within the public and not-for-profit sector operate within different contexts and under different pressures. This section identifies these pressures and opportunities, alongside a discussion of the types of activities that library and information managers within the various sectors are undertaking in order to meet these demands.

Higher and further education

> Increased levels of participation, widening access, pressure on human and physical resources, appraisal, audit and assessment has raised the profile of quality within higher education. (Harvey and Green, 1993, 9)

In both FE and HE institutions, rigorous audit and inspections have been introduced, for example Teaching Quality Assessment and the Research Assessment Exercise in the HE sector. The FE Funding Council has also developed explicit self-assessment criteria for colleges which have implications for the management and evaluation of college library services. These audits have been principally introduced by funding councils, whose role it is to ensure value for money and that standards are maintained across the sector. In some fields, such as medicine and law, external agencies are involved in setting appropriate academic standards.

These changes have undoubtedly impacted on the library and information services within these institutions. The 1993 Follet Report on library provision in the academic sector highlighted the need to address the management of information services, arguing that there were

> three areas where the review group consider that specific action will bring valuable benefits. These are strategic planning, and the context in which this needs to take place; the development and use of performance indicators and staff management. (Joint Funding Council's Library Review Group, 1993, 27)

Morgan (1995, 61) argues that, from the point of view of the practitioner, methods of performance assessment are vital in the management of information services. The evidence gained from the assessment can be used as a bargaining chip to maintain the standard of library services:

> With UK student numbers having increased by a massive 70% over the last
> six years, it is essential that mechanisms are in place to monitor and evalu-
> ate the library services so that highest standards of provision are maintained.

While there has been some debate about the value of quality management
procedures, practitioners have tended to adopt a pragmatic approach to
the new managerialism in the academic library sector. For example,
SCONUL has developed explicit assessment criteria for academic
libraries:

> Those managing academic libraries should accept the usefulness of man-
> agerial skills such as strategic planning. If they do so performance assessment
> will naturally become part of how they decide whether or not they are
> achieving their objectives. (Morgan, 1995, 47)

Within the FE sector the Council for Learning Resources in Colleges
(CoLRIC) was established as an independent support agency to offer
advice and guidance for the maintenance of library services. A key objective has been 'validating and auditing the quality of college learning
resource provision'. CoLRIC has also published a detailed pro-forma for
self-assessment against its peer-accreditation scheme for learning resource
centres.

Health sector libraries

The 1989 White Paper Working for patients held within it the foundation
of the most fundamental overhaul and reorganization of the National
Health Service since its inception in 1948. An internal market was to be
created which would separate the policy-making and management function
of the health service from its provision. Health authorities were given the
power to purchase the most cost-effective health-care provision available.
Contractual relationships were also established through the widespread
compulsory competitive tendering of catering, cleaning and laundry
services (Walsh, 1995). The understanding was that the introduction of
these business management practices: 'would facilitate savings which could
be reinvested in the service' (Kinnell and McDougall, 1997, 72).

These changes were introduced within the context of an increasing emphasis being placed on achieving patient satisfaction through, for example, the Patients' Charter. Again, the adoption of quality management principles and practices such as performance indicators and measures would provide the necessary evidence that health-sector services were continually improving their cost-efficiency and cost-effectiveness.

Health-sector libraries can be found in organizations across the public and private sectors, including academic institutions, local authorities, health-care trusts and the pharmaceutical industry. As a consequence, demands for cost-efficiency within all of these institutions have impacted on health library and information services. As the Library and Information Cooperation Council (LINC) Health Panel suggests:

> Health library and information services are facing increased scrutiny by their parent organizations in terms of value for money. (LINC Health Panel, 1997, ii)

They go on to claim that:

> Part of the quality improvement process is the development of standards that can be used to assess and support library and information services in providing cost-effective, client-centred services. (LINC Health Panel, 1997, ii)

To this end the LINC Health Panel accreditation working group developed explicit guidelines for the assessment of health-sector library services. The guidelines covered issues such as planning, customer satisfaction, resource management and performance assessment:

> experience of librarians involved in other accreditation systems indicates that the accreditation checklist must be accompanied by clear guidance for assessment, whether this is self-assessment, peer-assessment or external assessment. (LINC Health Panel, 1997, iii)

Civil Service

The Finance Management Initiative (FMI) was announced in May 1982; it aimed to improve financial-management practices in the Civil Service and to ensure value for money. In order to do this, Civil Service managers were asked to address three key issues: (Carter et al, 1992; Massey, 1993)

- that objectives for actions were set and appropriate performance measures derived
- that activities were costed and resources managed efficiently and effectively
- that managers were supported in their work through relevant information and appropriate training.

The FMI was perhaps the catalyst to many of the new business-management practices which were adopted within the Civil Service and the public sector, and in particular the use of performance indicators (Carter et al, 1992). The FMI also laid the foundations for the Next Steps Initiative, a programme which sought to devolve the service-delivery sector of national government away from the ministers who made policy decisions. Various institutions transferred to agency status including the Benefits Agency and the Driving Standards Agency; indeed, over 70% of the former Civil Service were employed in the new agencies. Ministers set key performance indicators for the agencies, in order to prove that they were providing an efficient and effective delivery of services.

The Office of Public Services (OPS) launched the Public Sector Benchmarking project in April 1996, piloting the Business Excellence Model in 30 organizations, principally Next Step Agencies. A second phase, April 1997-January 1998, expanded the use of the model to over 100 organizations, accounting for over half the workforce of the Civil Service. The aim of the project was to:

> support the government's continuing drive to achieve best value in the delivery of public services, by exploiting the value of benchmarking to support agencies and other public sector organisations, in meeting the challenge of improving the management of their operations within tight financial constraints. (Samuels, 1998, 1)

The research showed that while all of the agencies out-performed private sector organizations in customer focus, in other key areas such as leadership and employee management the majority did not compare well.

Public libraries

Like the higher-education sector, public libraries have faced a number of rigorous and far-reaching reviews in recent years which have challenged their current working practices and management procedures. The 1988 Green Paper *Financing our public library services* challenged the concept of free library services by identifying the provision of books and printed material as their core service; anything else was considered peripheral and libraries were encouraged to charge for these other services (Kinnell and McDougall, 1997). The Aslib Review for the Department of National Heritage took this re-evaluation of public library services a step further. The recent requirement to provide the Department of Culture, Media and Sport with annual library plans will undoubtedly lead to an interest in effective planning techniques. The advent of Internet access in all public libraries (Library and Information Commission, 1997) will also add to the challenges and opportunities public libraries face.

Public library authorities also operate within a local government context – library provision is the statutory responsibility of local authorities. As a consequence, library services have also had to face stringent budget cuts, contracting out, external audit and inspection in recent years. All of these changes have impacted on their interest in quality management. In 1998-9 many public library authorities have been piloting Best Value – an initiative which is likely to become a requirement for all local government services. Best Value encourages local authorities to demonstrate they are providing value for money and quality in the delivery of services.

Public library services have taken diverse routes to implementing quality management practices (Milner, Kinnell and Usherwood, 1997). However, a number of national initiatives have taken place which aim to provide evidence and promote the practice of excellent service delivery:

- CIPFA Plus surveys
- CIPFA Performance Indicators
- Public Library Quality Forum.

Recent developments

While it is not the aim of this chapter to discuss the various quality management tools and techniques used by the library and information profession, there have been a number of recent developments which are worth mentioning. These developments have been in the support tools which library professionals have been using to manage their services.

IT-based management systems

With the increasing use of IT in libraries, a number of projects have investigated the potential of IT-based decision-support systems for use in library and information services. The Concerted Action on Management Information for Libraries in Europe (CAMILE) project, funded by the European Commission, sought to:

- develop tools to support the decision-making process in academic and public libraries
- identify the impact of management information in library services
- identify methods of implementing management-information systems in library services
- identify means of assessing and developing appropriate performance indicators
- identify management-information tools
- identify decision support tools.

Four projects were developed under this framework:

- DECIMIL (Decision Making in Libraries) – identifying a decision support module for integration into library housekeeping systems
- EQLIPSE (Evaluation and Quality in Library Performance: System for Europe) – developing an IT-based system to support quality management and performance measurement
- DECIDE (Decision Support Model for European Academic and Public Libraries) – developing a decision support system for both automated and non-automated systems in academic and public libraries

- MINSTREL (Management Information Software Tools for Research in European Libraries).

Performance measures and indicators for the electronic library

The growing use of technology across the public library and information sector has led to the development of specific performance measures for the electronic library. A number of projects have sought to identify key performance indicators for assessing the effectiveness of the electronic library. These developments are vital if librarians are to secure and maintain funding for IT provision.

Government task force

In January 1999 the Cabinet Office announced a new task force which would investigate the potential of four quality management schemes that might contribute to the effective management of public sector organizations. These four schemes were:

- Charter Mark
- Business Excellence Model
- Investors in People
- ISO 9000.

The objective of the task force was to investigate links between these schemes in order to 'maximise their collective impact' (Cabinet Office, 1999) for the management of public services. The overall aim of the task force was to influence the White Paper *Modernising government*, published in spring 1999.

At the same time it was announced that the criteria for the Charter Mark were to be developed to include partnership working and consultation with front-line staff. The Cabinet Office also announced a publication (Cabinet Office Service First Unit, 1999) to help public sector managers decide which is the best quality management approach for their services.

Should these schemes become a statutory requirement, there will undoubtedly be a rise in the development and use of quality management initiatives within public sector information services. However, care must be taken to ensure that the nature and values of the public sector are secured in these implementations of quality management.

Conclusions

This chapter has shown that the ethos of economy, efficiency and effectiveness has had a significant impact on the way in which the public sector has been managed over the past two decades. In particular, it has led to the widespread implementation and use of quality management tools and techniques, many of which were founded in the private sector. However, these approaches to quality management have not accounted for the different characteristics of public sector customers. The notion of equity in service provision has been missing from many of these management theories and models. It has been shown that there is a real need to develop alternative models of good management practice in order to account for the various constraints currently faced by organizations in the public library and information sector.

References

Aslib (1995) *Review of the public library service in England and Wales for the Department of National Heritage: final report*, Aslib.

Audit Commission (1993) *Putting quality on the map*, Audit Commission.

Brockman, J (ed) (1997) *Quality management and benchmarking in the information sector*, Bowker-Saur.

Burton, C, Greenhalgh, L and Worpole, K (1996) *London: library city. The public library service in London: a strategic review*, Comedia.

Cabinet Office (1999) New quality scheme taskforce announced. Press release (January), CAB 23/99.

Cabinet Office Service First Unit (1999) *How to improve your services: a guide to quality schemes for the public sector*, Cabinet Office.

Carter, N, Klein, R and Day, P (1992) *How organisations measure success: the use of performance indicators in government*, Routledge.

Clayton, C (1993) Quality and the public services, *Public Library Journal*, **8** (1), 11-12.

Davies, A and Kirkpatrick, I (1995) Face to face with the sovereign customer: service quality and the changing role of professional academic librarians, *Sociological Review*, **15**, 782-807.

Dearing, R (1997) *Higher education in the learning society: report of the national committee*, HMSO.

Freeman-Bell, G and Grover, R (1994) The use of quality management in local authorities. *Local Government Review*, **20** (4), 554-69.

Garrod, P and Kinnell, M (1997) Towards library excellence: best practice benchmarking in the library and information sector. In Brockman, J (ed) *Quality management and benchmarking in the information sector*, Bowker-Saur.

Harvey, L and Green, D (1993) Defining quality, *Assessment & Evaluation in Higher Education*, **18** (1), 9-34.

Henty, M (1989) Performance indicators in higher education libraries, *British Journal of Academic Librarianship*, **4** (13), 177-90.

Joint Funding Council's Library Review Group (1993) *Report*, Higher Education Funding Council for England.

Jones, K, Kinnell, M and Usherwood, B (1999) *Planning for public library improvement: report of the second project workshop*, Department of Information and Library Studies, Loughborough University.

Kerslake, E and Kinnell, M (1996) *Report to the British Library Research and Innovation Centre: quality management for library and information services policy forum*. Department of Information and Library Studies, Loughborough University.

Kinnell, M (1995) Quality management and library and information services: competitive advantage for the information revolution, *IFLA Journal*, **21** (4), 265-73.

Kinnell, M and MacDougall, J (1997) *Marketing in the not-for-profit sector*, Butterworth-Heinemann.

Kirkpatrick, I and Martinez Lucio, M (1995) *The politics of quality in the public sector: the management of change*, Routledge.

Library and Information Commission (1997) *New library: the people's network*, Library and Information Commission.

LINC Health Panel (1997) *Accreditation of library and information services in the health sector: a checklist to support assessment*, LINC Health Panel Accreditation Working Group.

Linley, R and Usherwood, B (1998) *New measures for the new library: a social audit of public libraries. British Library Research and Innovation Centre Report 89*, Department of Information Studies, University of Sheffield.

McKevitt, D and Lawton, A (1996) The manager, the citizen, the politician and performance measures, *Public Money and Management*, **16** (3), 49-54.

Massey, A (1993) *Managing the public sector: a comparative analysis of the UK and US*, Edward Elgar.

Maxwell, R J (1984) Quality assessment in health, *British Medical Journal*, **288**, 1470-1.

Milner, E, Kinnell, M and Usherwood, B (1997) Quality management and public library services. In Brockman, J (ed) *Quality management and benchmarking in the information sector*, Bowker-Saur.

Morgan, C and Murgatroyd, S (1994) *TQM in the public sector: an international perspective*, Open University Press.

Morgan, S (1995) *Performance assessment in academic libraries*, Mansell.

Pfeffer, N and Coote, A (1991) *Is quality good for you?*, Institute of Public Policy Research.

Porter, L (1992) Quality assurance: going round in circles, *Aslib Information*, **20** (6), 40-241.

Samuels, M. (1998) *Towards best practice: an evaluation of the first two years of the public sector benchmarking project 1996-1998*, Cabinet Office Next Steps Team.

SCONUL (1992) *Performance indicators for university libraries: a practical guide*, SCONUL.

Stewart, J and Walsh, K (1989) *The search for quality*, Local Government Training Board.

Stewart, J and Walsh, K (1992) Change in the management of public services, *Public Administration*, **70**, 499-518.

Usherwood, B (1992) Managing public libraries as a public service, *Public Library Journal*, **7** (6), 141-5.

Usherwood, B (1996) *Rediscovering public library management*, Library Association Publishing.

Walsh, K (1991) Quality and public services, *Public Administration*, **69**, 503-14.

Walsh, K (1995) Quality through markets: the new public service management. In Wilkinson, A and Willmott, H (eds) *Making quality critical: new perspectives on organisational change*, International Thomson Business Press.

Wilding, P (1994) Maintaining quality in human services, *Social Policy & Administration*, **28** (1), 57-72.

Wilkinson, A, Redman, T and Snape, E (1993) *Quality and the manager: an IM report*, Institute of Management.

Wilkinson, A and Willmott, H (eds) (1995) *Making quality critical: new perspectives on organisational change*, International Thomson Business Press.

Wilkinson, A and Willmott, H (1996) Quality management, problems and pitfalls: a critical perspective, *International Journal of Quality and Reliability Management*, **13** (2), 55-65.

3
The push to self-assessment

Introduction

Given the seemingly widespread adoption of established quality management techniques such as standards, specifications and performance measures across the public sector, library and information managers might be forgiven for wondering what benefits new approaches such as self-assessment can provide for their organization. This chapter offers a critique of how traditional approaches to quality management have been applied within library and information services. It shows that, while there is a commitment to using more efficient management practices across the sector, in reality there are many internal and external factors which can impact on the successful adoption of such approaches. The discussion then turns to how self-assessment might help library and information managers address these issues, and goes on to examine the potential of such a management tool for library and information services.

Much of the discussion in this section is based on semi-structured interviews which were carried out within three demonstrator public library services, and an analysis of the extensive literature on the needs of library and information service managers in the face of demands for accountability to all their stakeholders. Those interviewed helped identify a number of issues which are impacting on the implementation of quality management procedures:

- the absence of a planned, coordinated structure or framework for implementing quality management initiatives
- the lack of internal and external communication strategies for quality management programmes
- the inconsistency in the deployment and use of initiatives, even within the same service structure
- the lack of appropriate monitoring frameworks for initiatives
- the dearth of adequate performance indicators or measures for employee, customer and stakeholder satisfaction
- the inadequacy of assessment strategies for initiatives
- the failure to ensure service reviews to inform the service planning process
- the negative impact of external pressures on library and information services, such as budget cuts and restructuring.

Planning ahead

> If we really wanted to encourage quality we would be starting from the ground up. It's quite obvious that even out there in the so called real world, businesses have opened up to the fact that it's not something that is added onto your service, it's something intrinsic to it. That's where we could make the difference. But we don't encourage quality because we see it as something that is imposed, an afterthought. (Interviewee, demonstrator service)

When considering how each of the demonstrator services approached the implementation of quality management, it soon became clear that there were critical issues which needed to be addressed in how this process was being managed. This was not just in terms of how these changes were being communicated to staff, but of how the actual approach was being planned and structured within the services.

Various factors had influenced the demonstrator services' decision to adopt quality management principles and techniques. Leading these factors was the desire to improve the way in which the services on offer to their users (customers) were managed. In part, this was due to the changing demands from senior managers and external stakeholders about the way in which the services should be managed. As local authority services, they were under pressure to demonstrate value for money and that they were accountable to their customers. Many of the initiatives adopted, eg comments cards and stock suggestion schemes, were identified with these requirements in mind. Indeed, recent research has shown that the majority of quality initiatives in place in public library authorities are related in some way to ensuring customer involvement (LGMB, 1997b).

Evidence from European colleagues also suggested that they were adopting quality management techniques to improve services for customers (Swedish National Council for Culture Affairs, 1995; IFLA, 1997), However, pressures at a local and national level were also playing an important role as a catalyst for quality improvement. A Dutch colleague suggested that direct access to the Internet was providing competition for library and information services: 'if we can't improve our services, we will lose our role in society'.

The demonstrator services were also keen to identify tools and techniques which would help them plan and manage more effectively. From the interviews and the literature it was clear that even before the rise in TQM many practitioners felt they were already implementing good practice (Lester, 1994). As one interviewee in library service C stated: 'I have always been involved in continuous improvement'. However, adopting a formal quality management programme offered a way of demonstrating this to external stakeholders.

Table 3.1 below shows how quality was managed within the demonstrator services prior to the implementation of the self-assessment. From the evidence of the research studies reported in Brockman (1997), it is clear that the piecemeal approach to quality which was evident here was also found in other sectors. Academic libraries, for example, had a wide range of attitudes to and practice of quality management (Garrod and Kinnell, 1997). Between 10 and 15 initiatives were identified in each service. These are summarized in Table 3.2.

In each of the services the initial imperative for quality had come from those in senior management positions, with front-line staff then playing some role in taking this forward. The amount of front-line influence in the development of the quality audit varied from service to service, although all managers recognized the need for front-line involvement and ownership, since these staff would be responsible for its implementation.

Table 3.1 *Management of quality in demonstrator services*

	library service A	library service B	library service C
initial quality driver	quality team	senior management team	client-side through contracts and specification
implementation structure	coordinated at departmental level	coordinated at departmental level	client-side informs business unit
	local initiatives	local initiatives	
initiatives in place	12 initiatives	15 initiatives	15 initiatives
monitoring of initiatives	5-part framework	building audits customer comments	customer comments
review of initiatives	monitoring informs review	monitoring informs review	informal approach
			client driven
how links to service planning	unclear how assessment informs planning	adopting structured feedback cycle	unclear how assessment informs planning

Table 3.2 *Initiatives identified in each service*

	library service A	library service B	library service C
mission statement	•	•	•
vision statement		•	
customer-satisfaction surveys	•	•	•
customer-needs surveys		•	
quality awareness training	•		•
customer-care training	•	•	•
training in quality tools and techniques			
quality steering group/committee	•		•
quality circles/quality action teams	•		
total quality management			
quality improvement projects		•	
performance measurement	•	•	•
quality standards	•	•	•
quality awards or prizes	•	•	
quality days	•		
benchmarking	•		•
monitoring visits	•	•	•
other: includes staff suggestion scheme	•	•	•

Library service A had seconded two front-line staff to join the senior manager who was investigating potential routes to quality. It was felt that this would foster a sense of 'ownership' of the initiatives at a local level. The development team chose standards as the most appropriate mechanism for implementing quality, and then went on to ensure that service specialists and front line staff played a role in their development.

Senior managers in library service B involved all levels of staff in local authority-wide customer-focus training. The training aimed to reinforce or improve staff relationships with customers. Alongside this, the service implemented a widespread review of the way in which management practices were supported within the service. While front-line staff had no formal input into the redevelopment of these processes, a number were involved as facilitators in the training programme. Their feedback provided the senior managers with an overview of immediate responses among staff to the changing direction of the library service.

The push for quality in library service C had also started with senior managers, and had been informed by the business unit's contract and specifications. Consequently, front-line staff had had little involvement in the development of the initial approach to quality which was adopted. However, they were involved in the quality manual which was developed to ensure a standardization of procedures across the business unit.

There was little evidence of an overall coordination of quality initiatives within any of the services. While they were able to produce documentation to illustrate their procedures and their commitment to providing an excellent service to customers, it was clear that none of the services was following a structured approach to achieving total quality. None of the demonstrator services had a documented quality policy in place, nor did they define what was meant by quality in the context of their service structures. Again, this finding is supported by evidence from the literature which suggests that few library and information services are implementing formal quality programmes (Porter, 1993; Milner, Kinnell and Usherwood, 1997; LGMB, 1997a).

It was also clear from the interviews that the demonstrator services had not implemented supporting structures for the management of the majority of their initiatives, such as aligning them to the plans, policies or strategies that were already in place. The Swedish library service was also unable to show how the quality initiatives fit within its planning process.

For example, while library service A was able to provide convincing evidence of a planned approach to implementing quality standards, interviewees were unable to show how other initiatives such as performance measures, which were also deemed part of their 'quality package', fit with these standards, and, more importantly, how they supported the overall management of the service.

Within the demonstrator library services, examples of well-structured or poorly managed initiatives could be found side by side, often coordinated by the same person or team. While some initiatives had targets and objectives attached, others lacked specific action points or accountabilities. It was also telling that in none of the services did any member of staff identify all of the initiatives that were in place. Again, this was due to the lack of coordinating structure or framework for the initiatives.

Part of the problem here is that many people involved in implementing quality management programmes fall into the trap of believing quality management is about what initiatives are in place, and not about improving the way in which the service is managed. As Gillman (1992, 17) suggests: 'quality management is a state of mind, not a set of procedures. The procedures do not underpin quality: they are an expression of it and show how it will be applied'. Library and information managers are generally more concerned with improving the management of quality, not the quality of management (Gilchrist and Brockman, 1996).

Unless those implementing the new activities ensure that they are aligned to organizational goals, integrated into normal routines and deployed effectively across the library service, these paths to total quality will undoubtedly fail. As Black and Crumbley (1997, 92) warn: 'if an improvement plan is parallel, tangential or peripheral to . . . business plans and cycles, then it is in danger of withering on the vine'. Self-assessment provides a framework for linking together existing initiatives and integrating them into normal working patterns. In effect, the model of good practice provides an umbrella for all of the activities which the library service undertakes; it offers a quick and simple reference point for understanding the relevance of activities.

Deployment of the strategy

Many of the initiatives identified by staff were either no longer in place, had fallen into abeyance or were not applied consistently across the service. Four reasons were given for this:

- Some initiatives, such as the *benchmarking* process in library services A and C, were one-off projects and were not meant to be continued.
- In some cases, such as the *monitoring visits* in library service B, the initiative had begun, but had then quickly lost momentum, and little work had since been undertaken. As one respondent commented, 'we are not very good at squaring the circle; we often begin new initiatives but then don't do much with them'.
- In each library service, interviewees were able to identify initiatives which had been put on hold while the library service adjusted to a period of change. In library service A in particular, *quality standards*, the cornerstone of their formal quality approach, had been suspended owing to service restructuring.
- The interest of individual managers in the initiative determined the effectiveness with which they were deployed. In each of the library services evidence showed that some staff had not implemented initiatives that were operating service-wide, or were showing little support for them.

The lack of consistency in the deployment of initiatives was an issue which each of the library services were aware of and keen to address. In particular they were concerned to identify mechanisms to share good practice across the whole library service. Evidence suggested that the lack of a supportive framework for managing initiatives meant that the demonstrator services were constantly reacting to change rather than anticipating it and identifying possible solutions. However, in some instances the ability to plan effectively was outside the control of the library service. For example, when library service A was faced with stringent budget cuts, certain options such as the closure of library services were not available, because of the influence of its elected members. The capacity of library services to influence change is an issue which is discussed further in Chapter 6.

The self-assessment process addresses how service initiatives are deployed. It examines how systematically the activity is practised across the service, and questions whether activities are implemented in all relevant areas. Evidence from this can help in the preparation of communication strategies, training sessions and service development plans. It is used as the mechanism by which the organization can check how consistent and cohesive are its plans, policies and strategies (Holloway, 1995).

Communication of the strategy

When discussing how the quality management strategy was communicated within each service, it was clear that each had attempted to inform staff about the new management practices that were being implemented. However, when discussing individual initiatives it was evident that many staff were unaware of issues relating to:

- the working procedures of the approach
- the raison d'être for the approach
- how the approach complemented other library-service activities
- the outcomes or results identified by those initiatives undertaking performance assessment such as employee surveys or performance indicators
- the review of initiatives
- how the library service informed external stakeholders about the initiatives that were in place and their outcomes.

As a result, staff tended to be cynical about the value of such initiatives, because the actions of those implementing the initiatives contradicted their importance. The lack of effective communication strategies meant that most staff were unaware of what was happening service-wide. They were unsure about how these initiatives fitted with the other activities of the service. Therefore anything with the 'quality' tag tended to be perceived as an add-on initiative, and not integral to the delivery of the library service. These activities were considered an extra burden, rather than fundamental to the efficient and effective delivery of library services.

Front-line staff had a poor knowledge of the initiatives compared with those in management positions. In many cases the initiatives were implemented by management groups within the library service and then cascaded down through the management structure. However, in some cases they were implemented without additional training. As a consequence, front-line staff were generally less sure of the details of the management, planning and evaluation of quality initiatives. Their view of quality was often tied to their own service point, ie those initiatives they were directly responsible for, and in many instances they still had difficulty identifying how these initiatives were reviewed or improved. Few, if any, front-line staff could identify an overall coordinating framework for their organization's approach to quality.

This lack of coherent or consistent approach to the dissemination of information relating to new and ongoing initiatives was again due to the lack of a structured planning process to support the implementation and deployment of the initiatives. Without a supportive framework in place, the demonstrator services were losing the opportunity to develop and improve services. In one library service, for example, the results of customer-satisfaction surveys were fed back to customers but not to staff. Posters summarizing the results were sent to branch libraries to display for customers, but there was no formal process for discussing or analysing the results with staff. The opportunity to identify links between the delivery of services and customer satisfaction was missed.

One issue that was raised in the interviews was the concept of different stakeholders of library and information services: in particular, how the library services communicated a commitment to quality to their stakeholders and ensured that their opinions were accounted for in service planning. The UK services' understanding of the concept of 'stakeholder' was less mature than their Swedish counterparts, particularly at front-line level. However, the idea that library and information services have a diverse range of stakeholders, all of whom will have different needs and expectations, is one which is becoming increasingly common (Brophy, 1997; Kinnell and MacDougall, 1998). Comments from the demonstrator authorities showed that they were particularly keen to identify ways in which to balance these often conflicting demands. As one senior manager in library service B commented: 'it is not a term that we are used to; however, we need to take it on board for political reasons'.

Self-assessment enables organizations to identify such gaps in communication strategies. It provides a framework for understanding the relevance of initiatives. It expects organizations to address issues such as:

- how results are fed back to internal and external stakeholders
- how activities and procedures are documented and communicated to staff.

It provides managers with the opportunity to learn about the organization's activities in a structured and coherent way. As Holloway (1995, 405) suggests: 'a well-managed self-assessment process inevitably involves teams and individuals, throughout all levels, giving them ownership, creating an opportunity for education and awareness raising, and instilling the habit of assessing for managing improvement'.

Monitoring the strategy

There was conflicting evidence for just how systematic the monitoring and review of initiatives was in each of the demonstrator services. Indeed, this was one of the key areas where these services felt that they were currently failing to implement a successful approach.

In library service A, while there was a formal monitoring framework in place for its quality standards, there was none attached to other initiatives. Much of the standards monitoring had fallen into abeyance as a consequence of service restructuring. However, it was due to come back online during the course of the project.

Library service B did not have a formal monitoring programme for its quality initiatives. This was something that they were keen to adopt in the new service-support programme; as one senior manager commented: 'we desperately need a system for feedback which gives us a framework to manage the process for continuous improvement. If it [the new support initiative] doesn't work we need to make it work or do something else. It's important that we assess it from that point of view.' However, when asked about the targets against which the initiative would be monitored, the interviewee commented: 'I have personal aims which I think are system aims as well.' Again, the rhetoric of wanting to improve services systematically was not matched by the reality of day-to-day administration of projects. The mechanisms for monitoring the initiatives were not documented.

Library service C was in the process of revising its monitoring framework. At the time of the quality audit, one senior manager commented: 'I think we would be struggling to say that they are monitored as quality initiatives. There is a lot going on, but not in a coherent way.' The client-side was working with the business–unit to develop a self-monitoring process for routine library procedures. The business-unit had tended to respond to monitoring from the client-side, rather than build in its own mechanisms. As a consequence it was not always clear whether business-unit led initiatives had monitoring guidelines built in.

However, while monitoring initiatives provides evidence for understanding how systematic their deployment was, there is a danger that library services will fall into the trap of monitoring the implementation of initiatives rather than assessing their effectiveness. In a recent review of the changing practice in the local government sector, one commentator argued:

> [Quality] approaches seem to have settled, rather than to have continued to change, despite some quite negative responses to the adequacy of performance evaluation. (LGMB, 1997a, 48)

Assessment of the strategy

The effectiveness of the internal assessment of service achievements is another facet of library and information management which has been criticized in recent years:

> Library managers have come to realise that much of the data they collect relates to inputs and outputs. It does not provide information about the degree to which the library is achieving desired results. (Jurow, 1993, 113)

Morgan (1995, 47) argues that within the academic library sector, systematic performance assessment is 'regarded as too time consuming and a low priority'. From the interviews it was clear that although many initiatives and approaches had been implemented in the push for quality - such as standards, specifications, training programmes and service charters – the majority had been implemented without rigorous performance measures or targets attached. The interviewees in the demonstrator services highlighted two key issues which affected the internal assessment of initiatives:

• the lack of adequate indicators with which to identify the internal and external impact of the library service
• the unstructured approach to service assessment.

While one of the demonstrator library services was a dual recipient of the Charter Mark, it was clear that there was a recognition shared among all the services that the assessment of their activities was not well developed. They were especially concerned when considering the impact of the service on internal or external stakeholders. Part of this problem manifested itself in the lack of available performance indicators relating to:

• employee satisfaction
• customer satisfaction
• impact on society.

This dearth of indicators on the value of library services, Matarasso (1998, 49) suggests, has led to the situation that 'when librarians are asked to justify their work, the data is simply not there'. Library and information managers have tended to rely on performance indicators, such as stock turnover or stock per head of population, yet these assessments tend to 'measure what is measurable but miss what is important about the service' (Usherwood, 1998, 28). Qualitative approaches such as the social audit technique proposed by Linley and Usherwood (1998) can enrich the evidence on the value and impact of library and information services. Using a combination of qualitative and quantitative techniques, stakeholders can be provided with a real and valid account of what the library and information service has achieved (Usherwood, 1998).

However, even when performance targets were set, it was not always clear where the justification for targets lay, as the extract from one service's development plan suggests:

Increase membership. The target was a 10% increase. It was my target: I made it up, and have regretted it ever since. It has not been achieved. Membership has actually decreased by 1.4%.

Part of this problem lies with the way in which library services were planned and assessed. The links between service inputs and service outputs were rarely identified. For example, in library service C, customer standards were implemented alongside customer satisfaction surveys, but the surveys did not ask questions about perceptions of the library service's compliance with standards. This crucial flaw meant that each library service's approach was weakened overall.

The process of self-assessment addresses the objectives of the library and information service, the necessary actions to achieve them, and the evidence required to prove they have been met. Explicit links between what is planned and what is achieved are required (Brereton, 1996). One of the key benefits of self-assessment is that it provides 'the link between what the organisation needs to achieve and how it puts in place strategies and processes to deliver its objectives' (BQF, 1997, 5). In effect, it expects the organization to provide evidence that any performance indicator is adequate, relevant and rigorous enough for the task.

Review of the approach

A continuing criticism levelled at the use of quality management initiatives in the public information and library sector is that many of the activities are based on private sector approaches which have been uncritically applied (Milner, Kinnell and Usherwood, 1997). While it is true to say that all of the demonstrator library services attempted to identify approaches to quality which reflected their management culture and ethos, there is some doubt as to whether these approaches were adequately assessed for their suitability and applicability for the task in hand once they had been implemented. In particular, it was difficult to identify how the activities undertaken by the demonstrator services were reviewed and improved. Where initiatives were assessed, there was no system in place to ensure that the results led to improvements.

Some of the issues relating to service review and improvement have already been touched on in the previous sections. However, two critical issues were raised when discussing how the library services undertook their assessment of service achievements:

- The appropriateness and effectiveness of assessment tools were not identified.
- In all the library services there were no mechanisms to feed service performance data back into the planning process.

While each of the demonstrator services were involved in some form of assessment of customer perceptions of the library service, they were critical of the value that such an approach could offer, because customers had a relatively low expectation of what the service could provide. As a senior manager in library service A stated: 'the problem with asking people what they want is that they don't always know what they want'. These low user expectations were evident in the *Review of the public library service in England and Wales* (Aslib, 1995). In other instances, such as academic libraries, user expectations might be unreasonably high (Davies and Kirkpatrick, 1995). However, research also suggests that targeted user education programmes can help manage user expectations (Garrod and Kinnell, 1997).

Only one of the demonstrator library services undertook any direct assessment of employee satisfaction, and none of the services formally identified other stakeholder perceptions of library service achievements. The library services tended to rely on more traditional forms of service evaluation, eg comments cards and satisfaction surveys. However, they were all keen to explore the potential of alternative methods such as focus groups and forums. It was clear from the interviews that none of the services assessed the appropriateness and effectiveness of the mechanisms they used to undertake service evaluation. While they were all generally critical of traditional satisfaction surveys, they had yet to undertake any formal work to identify more effective methods, or to ensure that the assessment approaches they used were implemented efficiently and effectively.

Another issue which the library services acknowledged required attention, was the lack of formal mechanisms in place to ensure that service results were fed into planning and improvement cycles. The lack of an effective planning structure meant that even when appropriate data were available it was not clear how systematic was the process of feeding the results into the planning cycle.

Self-assessment can provide a suitable foundation for managing by fact. It provides the relevant evidence for the identification and targeting of potential improvement opportunities. The underlying assumption of the approach is that evidence-based management is a more effective approach to decision-making (Conti, 1997). It ensures that links between service achievements and service improvements are identified. In effect, self-assessment provides a mechanism for ensuring that the organization can readily identify the 'why and wherefore' for all of its activities.

The impact of external factors

The question of how easy it was to maintain the impetus in quality improvement programmes in the face of increasing pressure on public sector organizations was also raised during the interviews.

Between them, the library services were facing restructuring, budget cuts and local government review during the self-assessment process. The literature highlights two views of the place quality management might have in such a situation. One position argues that total quality has no place in organizations facing constant change:

> TQM does not readily blend in with wave after wave of restructuring, downsizing and re-engineering. (Anonymous, 1995)

The other argues that it provides an anchor in turbulent times:

> Far from total quality being difficult to maintain in a turbulent time, it provides an anchor and a route for managing through significant problems in ways which enhance staff understanding and maintain their commitment. (Hawkey, 1993)

Library services recognized the importance of quality, but were concerned about the impact on staff morale in the face of such drastic changes. As one senior manager in library service A commented:

> The problem is that we're trying to motivate and manage staff in the face of downsizing and cut-backs. We are having to explain ourselves to a wide range of people. The morale of the department is a key issue. The change is breeding cynicism . . . we're losing those staff with experience.

European colleagues also reported similar challenges: they were also facing budget cuts, increased public sector accountability and restructuring, and were therefore keen to identify mechanisms which would help them plan more effectively.

It was interesting to note that, owing to the amount of restructuring and change in each of the organizations, the development of quality initiatives had fallen into abeyance. Self-assessment gives useful evidence for the focusing of often scarce resources. Many of the concepts and techniques inherent in self-assessment are the basic tenets of good management practice.

Reasons for undertaking self-assessment

Discussions with the demonstrator library services provided a useful basis for understanding their initial reasons for wishing to undertake self-assessment. Services A and C indicated that they wanted to identify a mechanism with which to refocus and relaunch their approach to achieving total quality. Service B, on the other hand, had only recently begun its quality management programme, and was mainly concerned with identifying an accurate and valid assessment of its progress.

There was already some interest in, and understanding of, self-assessment techniques among the demonstrator services. Indeed, one library service had already identified a formalized self-assessment process as a long-term objective.

Library service A had been formally involved in quality management since 1992. Since then it had implemented over 30 quality standards through a well-defined management and monitoring framework. The service had already enjoyed external recognition of its quality programme as a dual recipient of the Charter Mark, and had earmarked the adoption of the EFQM Business Excellence Model as a future goal. However, the library service had recently undergone service restructuring which had resulted in the development of its formal quality programme falling into abeyance. At a local level, though, many initiatives and standards were still being implemented. Much of the project discussion with senior managers was dominated by the fact that the library service had also been targeted with a considerable budget cut, resulting in a 50% cut in all library opening hours. During the course of the research one-third of the existing county would form a new unitary service, and the remaining library service was then likely to be repositioned within the corporate structure. Consequently, representatives from the library service were concerned that, given the amount of change they were facing, self-assessment might not be a viable option at this stage, not least for its impact on staff morale.

The impact of quality management on staff was also a concern for library service B. Its formal approach to quality was still in its initial stages and the service was keen to identify quick benefits and long-term strategies for improvement.

Library service B had recently begun changing the culture and focus of the library service. The aim was to become more customer friendly rather than process-oriented, and to concentrate on providing an excellent service to local citizens. Keeping all staff on board was considered a critical issue. All staff in the service had undergone 'customer focus' training, with varying degrees of success; the Chief Librarian commented: 'many staff are not aware of the urgency to change the culture of the library service'. The service was also redeveloping its management-support services, and was attempting to change its management style from a reactive culture to a proactive culture. New initiatives were being brought on board to develop a means for long-term and short-term planning.

Library service C was interested in refocusing the way in which it managed its approach to quality. This service was working within a purchaser/provider corporate structure. The purchaser (client-side) wished to examine whether self-assessment would be a useful tool for refocusing working arrangements with the provider side (business unit).

The client-side in library service C was keen to develop a partnership approach, working with the business unit in the delivery of customer services. It had identified significant flaws in its monitoring framework and was therefore keen to relaunch its approach.

Work undertaken with the demonstrator services showed that self-assessment had the potential to play a key role in helping them to foster the planned and systematic approaches to continuous improvement they desired. They were keen to address the key issues of the planning, deployment and review of service initiatives, and this is what self-assessment enables organizations to address within a framework of good practice.

Recent research (Reed, 1997) on the fit between self-assessment and the public sector has highlighted a number of reasons for growing public sector interest in the concept of self-assessment:

- It offers a framework of best management practice for the sector.
- It offers a framework for organizations wishing to identify their achievements.
- It offers a framework for undertaking internal comparisons.

Summary

It was clear from this analysis that the demonstrator library services required further support in both implementing and sustaining quality management, and that self-assessment techniques had considerable potential at all stages in the planning and delivery of services. First, self-assessment provides a useful diagnostic tool for the management of library and information services. The model the organization is assessed against provides a detailed description of good practice. The assessment enables the organization to identify the areas in which it is not performing well. In particular, the assessment addresses the effectiveness of the planning approach, the consistency in service deployment, and the rigour and results of service review.

The process enables organizations to discover what they have achieved in relation to what they set out to achieve, as well as to identify the difference between perception and fact in relation to their results: in other words, the difference between what they think they have achieved and what they have actually achieved.

The British Quality Foundation, the organization charged with the promotion and development of the Business Excellence Model in the UK, has identified a number of potential benefits which can be derived from such a self-assessment process (BQF, 1997, 5):

- Self-assessment against models of good practice provides a rigorous method and a structured foundation for achieving continuous

improvement.
- Self-assessment against models of good practice provides a framework for linking together existing quality initiatives within organizations, and integrating them into normal working patterns.
- Self-assessment provides a structured approach to identifying current strengths and areas for improvement within organizations, in services offered and in management practices.
- Self-assessment provides a snapshot of where the organization is in relation to where it wants to be.
- Self-assessment provides the organization with an idea of where to focus resources; it aids business planning.
- Self-assessment provides a means of benchmarking the organization's achievements against both internal targets and external best practice.

In addition the British Quality Foundation (BQF, 1997, 5) claims that, when assessments are made against models of good practice, such assessments:

- will be based on concrete data as well as the perceptions of stakeholders
- provide consistency of direction and consensus of purpose
- provide a means of measuring progress over time.

Conclusions

This chapter has shown that, while many public library and information services have successfully implemented quality management initiatives, evidence suggests that they have had difficulty in maintaining and sustaining these programmes. Part of this problem has stemmed from the fact that the approaches they have implemented were not tailored sufficiently to their requirements. Other issues include the need to ensure that initiatives are fully integrated into normal working practices and routines, and are deployed effectively across the library and information service. In some instances practitioners have failed to realize that good practice cannot be achieved immediately; the key is understanding that improvements can be incremental as well as rapid.

Evidence suggests that self-assessment offers a means of identifying the value-added aspects of library and information services. However, the model of good practice that these services are assessed against must enable managers to develop strategies and contingencies for managing change. A model which provides guidance on where cuts and savings could be made will provide a degree of stability to counterbalance the uncertainty that comes with restructuring and budget cuts. It should also provide a framework for managing the often conflicting demands of various stakeholders. The next chapter brings many of these ideas together by offering detailed criteria for assessing the management practices of library and information services.

References

Anonymous (1995) The straining of quality, *The Economist*, (14 January), 65.

Aslib (1995) *Review of the public library service in England and Wales for the Department of National Heritage: final report*, ASLIB.

Black, S A and Crumbley, H C (1997) Self-assessment: what's in it for us?, *Total Quality Management*, **8** (2/3), 90-3.

BQF (1997) *Guide to self-assessment: public sector guidelines*, British Quality Foundation.

Brereton, M (1996) Introducing self-assessment - one of the keys to business excellence, *Management Services*, **40** (2), 22-3.

Brockman, J (ed) (1997) *Quality management and benchmarking in the information sector*, Bowker-Saur.

Brophy, P and Coulling, K (1997) Quality management in libraries. In Brockman, J (ed) *Quality management and benchmarking in the information sector*, Bowker-Saur.

Conti, T (1997) *Organisational self-assessment*, Chapman & Hall.

Davies, A and Kirkpatrick, I (1995) Face to face with the sovereign customer: service quality and the changing role of professional academic librarians, *Sociological Review*, 782-807.

Garrod, P and Kinnell, M (1997) Towards library excellence: best practice benchmarking in the library and information sector. In Brockman, J (ed) *Quality management and benchmarking in the information sector*, Bowker-Saur.

Gilchrist, A and Brockman J (1996) Where is the Xerox Corporation of the LIS sector?, *Library Trends*, **43** (3), 595-604.

Gillman, P (1992) Snares and delusions: the mis-management of quality. In *Total Quality Management: the information business: key issue 92*, University of Hertfordshire Press.

Hawkey, P (1993) Foot down on the quality drive, *Local Government Chronicle*, (30 April), 14.

Holloway, B (1995) Gaining the benefits of self-assessment, *Quality World*, (June), 404-6.

IFLA (1997) *National reports on performance measurement and quality management in public libraries. IFLA Satellite Meeting August 25-28, 1997*, Zentral- und Landsbibliothek Berlin - Stadbuchereien, Dusseldorf - Deutsches Bibliothekinstitut.

Jurow, S and Barnard, S B (eds) *Integrating total quality management in a library setting*, The Haworth Press, Inc.

Lester, D (1994) *The impact of quality management on the information sector: a study of case histories*, EUSIDIC.

Kinnell, M and MacDougall, J (1997) *Marketing in the not-for-profit sector*, Butterworth-Heinemann.

Linley, R and Usherwood, B (1998) *New measures for the new library: a social audit of public libraries. British Library Research and Innovation Centre Report 89*, Department of Information Studies. University of Sheffield.

LGMB (1997a) *Portrait of change*, Local Government Management Board.

LGMB (1997b) *Quality initiatives: report of the findings from the 1997 survey of local authority activity*, Local Government Management Board.

Matarasso, F (1998) *Beyond book issues: the social potential of library projects*, Comedia.

Milner, E, Kinnell, M and Usherwood, B (1997) Quality management and public library services. In Brockman, J (ed) *Quality management and benchmarking in the information sector*, Bowker-Saur.

Morgan, S (1995) *Performance assessment in academic libraries*, Mansell.

Porter, L (1993) *Quality initiatives in British library and information services. British Library Research and Innovation Centre Report 6105*, BLRIC.

Reed, D (1997). *Public sector excellence research report*, British Quality Foundation.

Swedish National Council for Cultural Affairs (1995) *Evaluating the GOK project: the innovative capacity of the Swedish library system*, Statens Kulturrad.

Usherwood, B (1998) Much more than numbers, *The Bookseller*, (8 May), 28-9.

4

Self-assessment criteria for library and information services

Introduction

The previous chapter offered suggestions as to why library and information services would seek to undertake self-assessment. The desire to identify and benchmark examples of good management practice was inherent in many of the suggestions offered by library services. Self-assessment is generally carried out against a model of good practice. This model summarizes the issues which organizations must consider. Often, explicit assessment criteria are derived from the model, which provides the means to make a more robust and comprehensive assessment. This chapter outlines the self-assessment model and the criteria which have been derived for the library and information sector. The inherent management principles and core values of the model in the context of the library and information sector are described first, and then guidelines for understanding the criteria and examples of appropriate evidence are provided.

The Library and Information Sector Improvement Model (LISIM)

The Library and Information Sector Improvement Model was developed as a model of good management practice for library and information services.

Management practices in ten key areas are summarized and defined. Comments from the demonstrator services and senior library and information practitioners were used in the development of the model. These discussions identified a number of issues which they felt should be accounted for in a model of library and information service improvement (Jones, Kinnell and Usherwood, 1998; Jones, Kinnell and Usherwood, 1999):

- The model should offer a supportive framework or structure for understanding the often disparate management activities in library and information services.
- The model should not merely summarize best practice, it should offer guidance on how library and information services can improve their current management practices and achieve excellence. Therefore the model should offer a staged approach to continuous improvement, with links between the stages identified, and guidance offered for moving up the model.
- There needed to be explicit links between the planning of the service and the assessment of its impact. The whole management cycle should be accounted for in the model - planning of services, their implementation, their review, and their improvement (plan-do-check-act).
- The model should take account of changing service structures within their various institutional contexts.

The LISIM offers particular relevance over other public sector models in three key areas:

- the added emphasis on systematic management of customer-facing services
- the need to address the wider impact of the library service on society- a potentially useful political tool
- the changing local and national pressures on the library and information sector in the UK, such as Department of Culture, Media and Sport planning guidelines, Best Value and the expanding use of Information Technology in libraries.

The model is shown in full in Section 3 of the resource pack, and is summarized in Figure 4.1.

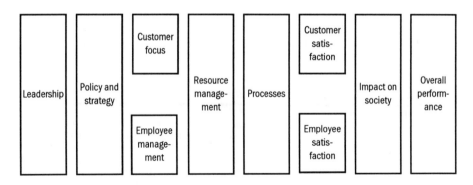

Fig. 4.1   *Summary of the LISIM (Source: demonstrator service B)*

The model has been well received by many library and information practitioners who view it as a useful service planning and development tool. They feel it has the potential of offering a framework for the efficient and effective management of library and information services. It also supports cross-sector benchmarking through the provision of detailed self-assessment criteria which are described later in this chapter (Jones, Kinnell and Usherwood, 1999).

Management principles of the LISIM

Chapter 2 showed that across the public library and information sector there is increasing pressure on professionals to adopt private sector management principles and techniques in the running of public services. Discussions with the demonstrator library services showed that there was an increasing willingness to use these techniques in the day-to-day administration of services, although there was some scepticism about the language which came with them. In particular the terms 'stakeholder' and 'benchmarking' caused the most concern. In many instances the ideas were already in use, for example fact-based planning was in use but the corresponding jargon phrase 'management by fact' was unfamiliar.

In order to secure professional acceptance it was necessary to identify some inherent principles which would act as a foundation for the structured approach to improvement which was defined in the model. This took the form of a variety of techniques which the library services would have to employ or address in order to improve their standing against the model. These principles were derived from the analysis of the core values identified by the demonstrator services. They are summarized in Table 4.1.

Table 4.1 *Inherent principles of the LISIM*

General principle:	Non-prescriptive	While the model presents criteria for assessment and offers examples of good practice, it does not prescribe the approach which the library and information service should undertake. It offers a broad spectrum of issues which might be considered, but it is up to the service in question to determine how relevant these are in the context of their own plans, policies and strategies.
Management principles:	Consistency of purpose	All plans, policies and strategies should be deployed in a structured and systematic way across the whole organization and all its activities should be coordinated and aligned to them.
	Continuous improvement	Continuous improvement should be the focus of all work practices and procedures and should be embedded in the culture of the service. Assessment measures should be aligned to goals, targets and objectives in order to facilitate a structured and systematic approach to continuous improvement. Excellent organizations are expected to provide evidence of year-on-year improvements in key result areas. Continuous improvement is also about using the review and assessment process to drive improvement.
	Benchmarking	Excellent organizations are expected to benchmark key result areas and be able to provide evidence of an improving trend when compared with good practice organizations. Excellent organizations are also expected to provide evidence of how they have used process benchmarking to drive improvements.
	Management by fact	Relevant and accurate information should be the basis of planning and improvement decisions within the service.
Human factors:	Visible and visionary leadership	The commitment of senior management is vital to the success of self-assessment. They drive the planning and improvement activities of the organization.
	Stakeholder consideration	Meeting the needs and expectations of external stakeholders is inherent in the model. Instead of focusing inwards, the service should be addressing the management of customer-facing services. The stakeholders of a service are those people or organizations who have a stake in the service. 'Stakeholders do more than simply use the library: they care about its success, they promote its activities, and they are lobbyists on its behalf' (Weingand, 1997, 58).These might include: staff, customers, councillors, council departments, funding councils, book suppliers, electronic information providers and library networks such as EARL, JANET, SELPIG.
	Employee development, involvement and satisfaction	The delivery of quality services is dependent upon motivated and committed employees. Therefore systems should be put in place to ensure that they are supported in their role.

Three different concepts were accounted for in the grounding principles. First was the desire to have an overarching principle that the library and information service should retain a high degree of autonomy in the way in which it approached self-assessment. Some library and information services may prefer to use the model as a service-development tool rather than as a mere performance measure. Therefore the model must not dictate too far what approach the library service should take in achieving best practice. The underlying principles also had to take account of the human processes involved in the model: the leaders who would drive the assessment, the employees who would implement it, and the external stakeholders who are the catalyst for service improvement.

The structure of the LISIM

The LISIM is presented as a model which summarizes ten core management practices in six stages of achievement. These achievement stages offer guidance on how the library and information service might improve its current approach. The model provides a useful basis for post-assessment planning by summarizing stages of organizational excellence and the approaches required to achieve them. These stages are summarized in Table 4.2. Figure 4.2 summarizes the planning and improvement mechanism the library service must implement in order to advance through the stages.

Table 4.2   *Stages to excellence on the LISIM*

Stage to excellence	Description
Baseline approach	No structured activity to improve current practice is undertaken.
Organizational commitment	The organization recognizes the need to address this area and begins planning an approach.
Planned implementation	Relevant management data are used to inform planning. Targets for improvement are set.
Systematic review	Success against targets is regularly reviewed and used to inform planning.
Ensuring consistency	Every effort is made to ensure that all plans, policies and strategies across the service are aligned.
Achieving excellence	Evidence shows that the organization is best in class.

The ten core management practices or criteria summarized in Figure 4.1 are discussed in Section 2 of the resource pack. For a fuller explanation readers are referred to the self-assessment criteria described in Section 4 of the resource pack. However, the model does offer an indication of the types of issues and questions which must be addressed in any library and information service wishing to adopt the LISIM as a framework for continuous improvement.

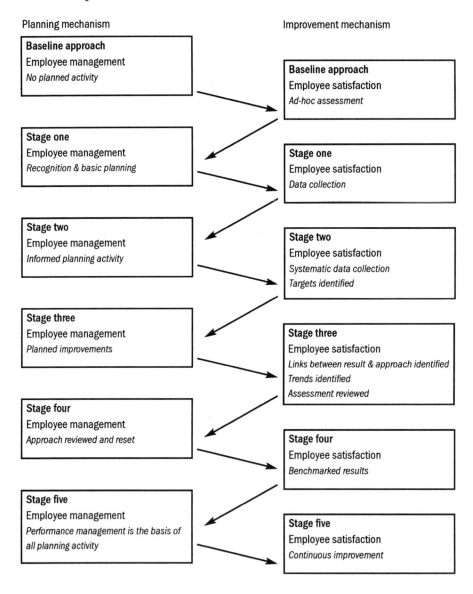

Fig. 4.2   *Mechanisms involved in improving one's position on the LISIM*

Understanding the self-assessment criteria

This section addresses the criteria which public library and information sector organizations will be assessed against. The LISIM summarized the types of issues that library and information services would need to consider in a self-assessment. However, in order to undertake a more effective assessment, explicit criteria were derived. The aim of this section is to examine the structure of the criteria, offer guidance for their interpretation and identify links between the criteria to facilitate the assessment process. Where relevant, examples of good practice are provided, as are detailed notes on the evidence which the assessment team needs to consider. The full criteria are listed in Section 4 of the resource pack.

The structure of the criteria

In its self-assessment the library and information service must address the ten criteria (leadership, policy and strategy, customer focus, employee management, resource management, processes, customer satisfaction, employee satisfaction, impact on society, and overall performance). These have been derived from the stages to excellence summarized in the LISIM. In order to facilitate the assessment, each criterion is split into a number of sub-criteria. In all there are 31 sub-criteria which must be addressed.

Table 4.3 *Links between the LISIM and the three assessment approaches*

LISIM criteria	Business Excellence Model	The Quality Framework	The Democratic Approach
Leadership	✓✓✓	✓	✓✓
Policy and strategy	✓✓✓	✓✓	✓✓
Customer focus	✓	✓✓✓	✓✓✓
Employee management	✓✓✓	✓✓✓	✓✓
Resource management	✓✓✓	✓✓	✓
Processes	✓✓✓	✓✓	✓✓
Customer satisfaction	✓✓✓	✓✓	✓✓
Employee satisfaction	✓✓✓	✓✓	✓✓
Impact on society	✓	✓✓	✓✓
Overall performance	✓✓✓	✓✓	✓✓

Key ✓✓✓ strong overlap ✓✓ some overlap ✓ little overlap

The criteria were derived from a detailed analysis of the three approaches to quality management outlined in Chapter 1. Table 4.3 shows how the criteria fit with the definitions of quality outlined in those approaches. The table shows that there are close links between the LISIM and the three approaches. During the work with the demonstrator services it became clear that the structure and framework of the Business Excellence Model had a great deal to offer the management and planning approaches of library and information services (Jones, Kinnell and Usherwood, 1998). These discussions also showed that the criteria need- ed to be tailored and adapted to reflect the needs of public library and information service organizations, a requirement that the two approaches outlined by Stewart and Walsh (1989) and Pfeffer and Coote (1991) could support. In particular, the demonstrator services were keen to develop criteria which would address their customer focus. They were also keen to identify mechanisms to evaluate their impact on society from the con- text of the library and information sector, eg on literacy and educational attainment. However, while there is a difference between the LISIM self- assessment framework and the general framework offered by the British Quality Foundation, by adopting a similar structure and addressing simi- lar issues, it will still be possible to benchmark achievements and share experience across the public sector.

The extract from the **leadership criterion** (Table 4.4) shows that wherever possible guidance is provided on the types of evidence which the service must endeavour to identify and consider in its self-assessment.

Table 4.4 . *The structure of the self-assessment criteria*

Criterion for assessment	Explanation
Leadership	CRITERION
Leadership (1a)	SUB-CRITERION
Evidence is required of how leaders create a culture which supports the pursuit of quality management within the service	Evidence required
Consider how senior managers:	
• drive the development, planning, implementation and review of the strategic direction of the service	Issue to consider
• define and communicate the strategic direction of the service	prompts for discussion
• define the values, objectives and direction of the service	prompts for discussion
• communicate the values, objectives and direction of the service	prompts for discussion

Each sub-criterion is further sub-divided into a number of issues to consider. The issue to consider is perhaps where the self-assessment process starts for the service. It is here that managers will need to address whether the relevant activities have been undertaken. As suggested in Section 1 of the resource pack, the types of issues to consider are not pre-scriptive and the service does not have to address each one. There may be valid reasons why certain activities are not undertaken. It is necessary, however, to identify this in the assessment. Appropriate reasons for exclusion might include:

- The sub-criterion may not fit within the management remit of the organization.
- The assessment team may decide that the activities are not a priority for the service eg monitoring strategies for non-users.
- Certain issues may be outside the control of the service, such as pro-curement regulations. However, if this is the case, then evidence is required about how the library and information sector feeds back into policy-making at a higher level.

Each issue to consider is expanded further with various prompts for dis-cussion. These are not listed in any order of preference, and are there to provide extra guidance in the self-assessment. Again, they are not meant to be prescriptive.

Reading through the assessment criteria it should become apparent that some refer to how the library and information service's activities are planned; these are commonly called 'enabler' criteria (BQF, 1997). Some criteria refer to the results or outcomes of these activities, and these are known as 'results' criteria (BQF, 1997). For example, the activities carried out in customer focus should provide indicators for the assessment of cus-tomer satisfaction. Table 4.5 shows the enabler and results criteria in the LISIM:

When assessing against the enabler criteria, the assessment team is looking for evidence relating to the planning, review and deployment of service initiatives – see Table 4.6.

Table 4.5 *The enabler and results criteria*

Enabler criteria	Results criteria
(What the service plans)	(What the service is achieving)
Leadership	Customer satisfaction
Policy and strategy	Employee satisfaction
Customer focus	Impact on society
Employee management	Overall performance
Resource management	
Processes	

Table 4.6 *Assessment against the enabler criteria*

Planning	That appropriate methods / tools / techniques are used in the planning of initiatives. That they are integrated into normal working practices. That the organization is seeking to prevent problems rather than deal with them.
Review	That reviews are planned and take place regularly. That the results of reviews are used to revise working practices.
Deployment	That service initiatives are implemented in all relevant sections and departments across the service.

When assessing the results criteria, the assessment team will be looking for evidence relating to the management of data collection. However, the critical evidence required will relate to the actual results, their review and scope – see Table 4.7

Table 4.7 *Assessment against the results criteria*

Results	Improving trends. That negative results or trends are acknowledged and acted upon. That targets are being achieved. That targets and trends are benchmarked. That results are caused by the approach.
Review	How results are fed back into the planning process.
Scope	That results cover all relevant areas of the organization. That a range of results are identified.

This evidence relates to the scoring framework of the Business Excellence Model (BQF, 1997). When undertaking the self-assessment it is suggested that the criteria are partnered. This will help the organization identify whether there are links between the planning, implementation, review and improvement of service activities. The appropriate partners are shown in Table 4.8

Table 4.8   Appropriate partners between criteria

leadership	overall performance
policy and strategy	impact on society
customer focus	customer satisfaction
employee management	employee satisfaction
resource management	processes

Exploring the criteria

Leadership

Strong leadership is the key to the effective management of library and information services. This issue has been identified in the Aslib review (1995) and has featured in other research reports on quality management for library and information services (eg Milner, Kinnell and Usherwood, 1997; Brophy and Coulling, 1997). Without the drive and determination of senior managers who can effect the necessary actions to develop and improve the service, then most improvement activities will fail (Frank, 1993). All three demonstrator authorities recognized the need for leadership, although they each offered differing perceptions on how this could be achieved. What was considered critical, however, was that senior managers understood the process of self-assessment and were supportive of its implementation. Research has shown that those organizations without an effective management structure and leadership tend to fare worse in all aspects of the self-assessment. Criteria relating to leadership are vital in self-assessment: 'it sets the stage for almost everything that follows; here the assessors will gain considerable insight into a company's commitment to TQM' (Foley, 1994, 49). The actions of senior managers are pivotal to an organization's ability to achieve continuous improvement.

For the first self-assessment, the leaders of the library and information service should be considered to be the chief librarian and the senior management team. A more robust assessment would also consider anyone in a management position within the service. However, as suggested in Chapter 5, first-time assessments are generally better suited to taking a general overview of the service rather than a comprehensive assessment.

While the assessment criteria in the toolkit are derived from the Business Excellence Model (BQF, 1997) in keeping with the specific context of public sector library and information services, these criteria were expanded in order to offer some critique of how senior managers affected and shaped the strategic direction of the service within its wider institutional context. Two key requirements of effective leaders were identified and summarized:

- Leadership (1a) How do senior managers create a culture for quality?
- Leadership (1b) How do senior managers promote quality outside the library and information service?

The leadership criterion requires the assessment team to consider how senior managers drive a service culture which supports the pursuit of quality management within the service, and how they promote a commitment to quality issues outside the service. These issues are dealt with in more detail below.

LEADERSHIP (1A) HOW DO SENIOR MANAGERS CREATE A CULTURE FOR QUALITY?

The assessment team should be looking for evidence of how senior managers are involved in developing the structure, culture and direction of the library and information service within its corporate context. Evidence is also required for how leaders drive the development, training, empowerment and recognition of staff across the service and how they are involved in improvement activities. Prompts for discussion include how senior managers support training activities through the provision of resources, how they listen to – and, more critically, act upon – employee suggestions, and how they take part in and support service improvements. Those library and information services where senior managers take a real interest in the day-to-day activities of the service are likely to be more productive and to score higher in areas such as employee satisfaction.

LEADERSHIP (1B) HOW DO SENIOR MANAGERS PROMOTE QUALITY OUTSIDE THE LIBRARY AND INFORMATION SERVICE?

Here it is the role of the senior managers in the external environment which is being assessed: how they develop and sustain relationships with customers, partners, elected members and suppliers. The move to cross-sector partnerships is an increasingly common facet of public-service provision. The assessment team should consider how service managers are involved in developing partnerships with, for example, other departments in their local-authority framework, or perhaps how they are involved in securing sponsorship or support from the private sector. Not only should senior managers take a lead role in the development of the service, evidence is required for how they take part in the development of the profession by influencing policy at a local and national level. Prompts for discussion include how leaders learn from other organizations.

For both leadership sub-criteria evidence is also required of how the actions of senior managers are reviewed and improved. Where evidence suggests that this review is based on preventing problems, rather than solving them, the service will score higher.

LINKS TO OTHER CRITERIA

Leadership has strong links to all of the other criteria in the self-assessment process, because the actions of senior managers will drive the whole direction of the library and information service. However, there are particularly strong links between sub-criteria (1a) and sub-criteria (2a), (4b) and (10a) and (10c).

EXAMPLES OF GOOD PRACTICE

- Senior managers attend, fund and lead training sessions for all levels of employees, showing that they have a commitment to the professional development of all staff and a belief in the importance of training programmes as a means of continuously improving the services offered to customers.
- Senior managers elicit comments from all staff, customers, partners and suppliers on their individual performance and the performance of

the service. In addition, they should show that their comments are acted upon and fed into improvement cycles.

- Senior managers are visible in their support of the library service. This might involve attending relevant committees, floor-walking and having an open door policy.

Policy and strategy

Having effective plans, policies and strategies in place is an increasingly important aspect of the management of the public library and information sector (St Clair, 1994; Spiller, 1998). Knowing what the service is attempting to achieve in the long and short term; what initiatives need to be implemented or maintained to ensure that objectives are met; and how these plans support the delivery of wider organizational goals, are the key to ensuring the efficient and effective management of resources (Milner, Kinnell and Usherwood, 1997). Discussion with the demonstrator services showed that the desire to improve planning activities was given less priority than the need to address human-resource requirements. However, given the impetus to annual business planning within library and information services in all sectors, they were still keen to assess their current management approaches to setting policy and strategy. The demonstrator library services were concerned with ensuring consistency in the development and deployment of plans, an issue which was highlighted in the initial work with the services (Jones, Kinnell and Usherwood, 1998). This criterion forms an umbrella for understanding all library and information service activities. The assessment team should be looking for evidence that all plans, policies and strategies are consistent and congruent (Foley, 1994).

The criteria for assessing policy and strategy were again informed by the Business Excellence Model (BQF, 1997). However, they were altered to emphasize the need to identify planning in context. That is how the policy and strategy of the library and information service enables the wider institution (eg a university) to achieve its goals. Three key assessment areas are identified:

- **Policy and strategy (2a)** How policy and strategy are planned
- **Policy and strategy (2b)** How policy and strategy are communicated

- **Policy and strategy (2c)** How policy and strategy are informed.

Assessment against this criterion expects the library service to consider how policy and strategy are planned systematically and appropriately, informed by relevant management information and communicated to all stakeholders. Equally important is the consideration of how the review of policy and strategy is fed back into improvement cycles.

POLICY AND STRATEGY (2A) HOW POLICY AND STRATEGY ARE PLANNED

The assessment team should be looking for evidence of how the library and information service plans and implements its policy and strategies. Critical issues to address include how the service ensures that all of its plans, policies and strategies are aligned, how long- and short-term goals are identified and balanced, and how appropriate performance targets and objectives are developed and reviewed. Discussion should focus on how internal and external stakeholders are involved in the planning process, eg through employee suggestion schemes, customer comments and community forums. Attention should also be given to how the planning process is reviewed and improved. Given that planning processes are increasingly being implemented in library and information services, this should provide a useful summary of the support mechanisms that are already in place.

POLICY AND STRATEGY (2B) HOW POLICY AND STRATEGY ARE COMMUNICATED

Critical to the successful implementation of strategic plans is how they are communicated to internal and external stakeholders. Here the assessment team requires evidence of how the library and information service communicates its plans, policies and strategies. For a public library service this will mean addressing how their annual library plans are presented to elected members, the Department for Culture, Media and Sport, customers and employees. This includes considering how employees are informed of their role in the delivery of plans and how their understanding of these plans is evaluated. Again, the assessment team must address how these activities are reviewed and improved.

POLICY AND STRATEGY (2C) HOW POLICY AND STRATEGY ARE INFORMED

Management by fact is a core value of the LISIM. Sub-criterion (2c) asks the service to consider what evidence it has to suggest that its policies and strategies are informed by relevant internal and external factors such as corporate strategies, government initiatives and legislation. There is also the opportunity to address how service performance data are used to inform service planning, an increasingly critical aspect of the planning process.

LINKS TO OTHER CRITERIA

There are clear links between policy and strategy and sub-criteria (3a), (4a) and (6a), which deal with how processes are planned, and with (7c), (8c), (9c) and (10c), which deal with the outcomes or results of the planning process.

EXAMPLES OF GOOD PRACTICE

- Having annual reports which review what the library service has achieved, how these achievements have been assessed, what improvement opportunities have been identified and how these will inform future planning strategies.
- Having communication strategies (eg briefing papers, newsletters, pamphlets) which ensure that all internal and external stakeholders are informed of what the service is attempting to achieve, how it will achieve its goals, how it will measure its success, and the role of the stakeholder in helping the service achieve its targets.
- Having an effective planning process in place which ensures that relevant information is available to support the planning process, ensuring that appropriate targets and benchmarks are set for service plans, ensuring that all plans are aligned within the library and information service and to the wider organization.
- Setting appropriate goals, targets, objectives, accountabilities and performance measures for all library and information service activities.
- Ensuring that all aspects of the policy process are reviewed and that actions for improvements are identified and implemented. This will include ensuring that current plans are reviewed for their effectiveness.

Customer focus

The use of the term 'customer' to describe the user of public services still causes widespread debate as to its accuracy and validity, because it defines an inherently financial arrangement. However, while the language may be disliked, the notion that public sector organizations exist to meet the diverse needs of society is paramount (Stewart and Walsh, 1989). To achieve this, services must be planned with these requirements in mind. However, there are issues to address, such as how the library and information service knows who its customers are, what efforts are made to ensure they are able to participate in the service decision-making process, and how the library and information service attempts to ensure equity in treatment (Pfeffer and Coote, 1991; Sirkin, 1993; Usherwood, 1998).

Although the Business Excellence Model stated that customer focus was an underlying core value in the model, explicit criteria relating to its implementation and use were not provided. Given that meeting 'customer' needs is the core activity of the public library and information sector it was decided to create a relevant assessment criterion. Discussions with the demonstrator library services showed that their staff were generally sceptical of the term 'customer'. They had adopted a fairly pragmatic stance towards its use within the local authority. While the library staff preferred to use the term 'borrower' to describe users, 'customer' was used by the majority of other services within the local authority. The customer focus sub-criteria were informed by the Democratic Approach to Quality (Pfeffer and Coote, 1991) and the Quality Framework (Stewart and Walsh, 1989). Feedback from demonstrator authorities was also used to determine the relevance of the sub-criteria and the activities used to determine good practice:

- **Customer focus (3a)** How customer services are planned
- **Customer focus (3b)** How customer services are managed
- **Customer focus (3c)** How customer services are communicated.

The assessment team must address how services are planned and developed with customer services in mind; how customer services are systematically and effectively managed, and how these services are communicated to customers.

Customer focus (3a) How customer services are planned

Here the assessment team will consider evidence relating to the planning of customer services. Evidence is required for how customers and non-users are identified and how customer needs and expectations are fed into the planning of services. The library and information service must also provide evidence that it ensures that all customers receive services appropriate to their needs, through, for example, the provision of short-loan collections, books on tape, mobile services and house-bound services. In effect, evidence is required for how all potential users of the service are accounted for in service planning. Mechanisms for ensuring customer participation in decision-making, and ensuring that all staff receive adequate customer-focused training, may also be considered under this sub-criterion.

Customer focus (3b) How customer services are managed

This sub-criterion addresses what mechanisms are put in place to support the management of customer services. Evidence is required for how the library and information service identifies and reviews customer-related goals and targets. The assessment team may also consider the setting of customer service standards and how service improvements are planned and targeted. Prompts for discussion include how the management structure of the library and information service supports the delivery of customer services and how customer-related goals and targets are aligned to appropriate policies and strategies.

Customer focus (3c) How customer services are communicated

A critical process in the delivery of customer services is their communication and marketing. Here the assessment team must consider evidence relating to how the library and information service ensures that customers are informed about what services are available, the service's desire to meet their needs, and how they can input into the service planning process. Part of the assessment should also include how these communication channels are reviewed for their effectiveness and how necessary improvements are implemented. Prompts for discussion include how a commitment to customers is communicated through the actions of staff, what mechanisms are in place to deal with customer comments and complaints, and how service performance is communicated to customers.

LINKS TO OTHER CRITERIA

The library and information service will also need to address how employees are trained to deal with customers (4d); how information provided to customers is managed (5c); and the assessment of customer services (criterion 7).

EXAMPLES OF GOOD PRACTICE

- Marketing strategies to ensure that all potential 'customers' are identified and appropriate services identified and promoted.
- Strategies to ensure that all potential customers are informed of their ability to participate in service-level decision-making, such as stock selection and opening hours.
- Statements relating to customer services, including aims, objectives and performance targets.
- A survey process which ensures that customer perceptions of the library and information service are identified and, where appropriate, fed back into improvement cycles.

Employee management

Many library and information services are now investigating initiatives such as Investors in People (IiP) as a potential supportive framework for managing employees (Goulding et al, 1999). The past few years have seen a rise in interest in initiatives for the development of public sector workers (LGMB, 1997). Organizations are moving away from management frameworks which dictate effective working strategies to employees, and towards systems which enable employees to participate in decisions about appropriate working practices. For example, Miller and Stearns (1994, 408) suggest that 'the heart and soul of quality improvement in an academic library is the empowerment of employees and . . . increased levels of participation'. A key requirement, therefore, is to ensure that there are strategies in place to enable employees to participate effectively, eg through training programmes (Jurow and Barnard, 1993). In discussion with the demonstrator library services, senior managers were quick to agree that the development and involvement of employees was a critical factor in developing the management procedures and practices across the service. However, in a number of key areas the rhetoric of wanting to involve employees in service development was often not implemented in practice.

The assessment criterion was derived from the Business Excellence Model (BQF, 1997), the Democratic Approach (Pfeffer and Coote, 1991) and the Quality Framework (Stewart and Walsh, 1989). However, the terminology was simplified to enable its wider application and use. The structure of the criterion was also altered to account for greater employee involvement, a factor that featured strongly in the discussions with the demonstrator authorities. Four critical issues (sub-criteria) were identified:

- **Employee management (4a)** How are human resources planned?
- **Employee management (4b)** How are human resources managed?
- **Employee management (4c)** How are employees involved in the library and information service?
- **Employee management (4d)** How are employees developed?

The employee-management criterion requires the assessment team to consider how the library and information service plans its human-resource strategies, how it involves staff in decision-making, how it facilitates the career development of employees, and what mechanisms the service has in place to manage its employees effectively. Evidence is also required for how the activities in this criterion link directly with the results from criterion 8, employee satisfaction. Critically, the library and information service should address how potential improvements are identified and fed into planning cycles.

EMPLOYEE MANAGEMENT (4A) HOW ARE HUMAN RESOURCES PLANNED?

The assessment team should be looking for evidence as to how the library service plans its human resource requirements; for example, how it identifies the skills and competencies required by its workforce to deliver its organizational goals, and how it structures and manages the recruitment and training process to account for these demands. Again, evidence is required for how human-resource needs are accounted for in all service plans, policies and strategies.

EMPLOYEE MANAGEMENT (4B) HOW ARE HUMAN RESOURCES MANAGED?

Here the assessment team will be addressing how effectively human resources are managed throughout the library service. Evidence is required for how the service adheres to key requirements such as equal opportunity and health and safety legislation. Issues to consider also include the effectiveness of management and working practices, and how these are both reviewed and improved. Prompts for discussion include the development and support of teams, whether relevant targets and priorities are set for improvement, and how the grievance process is managed.

EMPLOYEE MANAGEMENT (4C) HOW ARE EMPLOYEES INVOLVED IN THE LIBRARY AND INFORMATION SERVICE?

Here, evidence is required as to how the library and information service ensures that all employees are involved in service planning and improvement. Issues to consider here include how the employees are provided with relevant information in order to carry out their jobs efficiently and effectively, the effectiveness of internal communication strategies, and what mechanisms are implemented to support employee participation. Best-practice organizations will not only be able to provide evidence of employee participation through, for example, staff suggestion schemes, but also to provide additional evidence of targets and objectives for encouraging participation and - critically - how suggestions are acted upon.

EMPLOYEE MANAGEMENT (4D) HOW ARE EMPLOYEES DEVELOPED?

A critical factor in employee management is the development of employees through, for example, training programmes. Here, the assessment team must consider how effective the processes for developing employees are within the library and information service. Examples of relevant activities for consideration include mentoring programmes, career-development planning, appraisal schemes, training and skills needs assessments. Again, evidence is also required for how these practices are reviewed and improved.

LINKS TO OTHER CRITERIA

Issues relating to employee development and involvement are also covered in sub-criteria (1a), (2b), (2c), (3c), (5c), (6a) and (6b).

EXAMPLES OF GOOD PRACTICE

- Appraisal strategies which not only set targets for improvement, but address how the library and information service can help the development and empowerment of individual employees.
- Effective top-down and bottom-up communication strategies in place.
- Human-resources policies which are aligned to all plans, policies and strategies. The policies should cover issues such as recruitment and retention, induction, training, terms and conditions, relevant legislative requirements, and the exit process.
- A survey process which ensures that employees' perceptions of the library service are identified and where appropriate fed back into improvement cycles.
- A participation process which ensures the empowerment of individual employees. This will involve the setting of appropriate targets and performance measures.

Resource management

An efficient organization will have systems in place which ensure that financial information and physical resources and assets are efficiently and effectively managed (Brophy and Coulling, 1997). All public sector organizations are charged with delivering services in the most cost-effective way possible through, for example, Audit Commission and HEFCE requirements. To do this effectively, resources need to be managed to ensure value for money and the delivery of policy and strategy.

Discussions with the demonstrator authorities showed that, while they considered resource-management practices to be an important administrative consideration, they did not rate highly as a service issue.

The criterion for resource management was informed by the Business Excellence Model (BQF, 1997). Again, the structure was altered to take account of the requirements of the public library and information sector. Five key resource-related issues were summarized for inclusion:

- **Resource management (5a)** How are financial resources acquired and managed?
- **Resource management (5b)** How are assets managed?
- **Resource management (5c)** How is information managed?
- **Resource management (5d)** How is technology managed?
- **Resource management (5e)** How are relationships with suppliers and partners managed?

The resource-management criterion expects the assessment team to address how the library and information service manages its physical and financial resources and how relationships with suppliers and partners are developed, maintained and improved.

RESOURCE MANAGEMENT (5A) HOW ARE FINANCIAL RESOURCES ACQUIRED AND MANAGED?

Here evidence is required for how efficient and effective the management of budgets and financial resources is within the library and information service. Indicators of best practice include using budgets to inform and support service planning, identifying risk, and the review of procurement practices. Evidence is also required for how the library service secures alternative sources of funding, eg government initiatives, sponsorship and income generation. Again, a critical success factor is the review of financial management and planning to support improvement activities.

RESOURCE MANAGEMENT (5B) HOW ARE ASSETS MANAGED?

The assessment team should consider how buildings, stock and equipment are managed to support service delivery. Evidence is required for how physical assets are developed and managed in line with policy and strategy, for example, ensuring that the life-cycle of computer equipment is taken on board in information technology strategies. Other critical issues include having effective disaster-management procedures in place and ensuring that plans are in place for stock preservation and conservation. Evidence is also required as to how the environmental impact of the library service is accounted for, through, for example, energy-efficient light bulbs and low-radiation computer monitors. The assessment team may also consider any internal inspection practices, such as the use of building audits or monitoring visits. Finally, security procedures are also accounted for under this sub-criterion.

RESOURCE MANAGEMENT (5C) HOW IS INFORMATION MANAGED?

One of the eight core principles of the LISIM is management by fact. This sub-criterion relates directly to this principle by addressing how information is managed in the planning and delivery of services. Evidence is required for how the library and information service manages the internal planning of information through, for example, ISO 9000 procedures, information audits and procedures for handling confidential data. The assessment team is also expected to address these issues when considering how the information which supports staff in their work and the information passed to external stakeholders are managed.

RESOURCE MANAGEMENT (5D) HOW IS TECHNOLOGY MANAGED?

Information technology is playing an increasingly important role in the management and delivery of library and information services. This sub-criterion addresses how the service manages technology to support service delivery, not only to provide internal management information but also in customer-facing services. Here the critical issue is how appropriate technology is identified and implemented, and how these procedures are reviewed for their effectiveness.

RESOURCE MANAGEMENT (5E) HOW ARE RELATIONSHIPS WITH SUPPLIERS AND PARTNERS MANAGED?

Library and information services across the public sector are increasingly delivering services as part of a partnership approach such as urban regeneration programmes. Here the assessment team must consider how relationships with partners and suppliers are developed to improve the efficiency and effectiveness of resource management. Evidence is required as to how the library and information service ensures that its plans, policies and strategies are aligned with those of partner organizations to avoid duplication of effort. Evidence is also required for how the library service works with suppliers to maximize value for money in service delivery.

LINKS TO OTHER CRITERIA

The management of resources is also dealt with in sub-criteria (1b), (2a), (3a) and (4a).

EXAMPLES OF GOOD PRACTICE

- Having an IT strategy in place which covers issues such as appropriate levels of access, training requirements, funding, upgrading and security.
- Auditing buildings from the point of view of the customer, looking at issues such as cleanliness, guidance, signs, stock and displays.
- Having security arrangements in place, eg alarms, tags on books, anti-virus protection on computers.
- Ensuring that depreciation and maintenance requirements are accounted for in costing strategies.
- Maintaining a register of fixed assets and equipment.

Processes

The management of processes is integral to the delivery of library and information services (Brophy and Coulling, 1997). Having documented working practices and procedures in place enables standards to be supported across the service. While process management was not considered a prime core value by the demonstrator authorities, it was perhaps the most fundamental criterion in the LISIM. As Barnard suggests (1993, 66): 'Identifying and evaluating the critical processes that drive an organisation is vital to the continuous improvement of systems fundamental to TQM'. This criterion provides the link between the planning of services and its potential outcomes; for example, how the cataloguing process can impact on customer satisfaction – customers might find the classification confusing. Typical library and information sector processes include cataloguing and indexing, interlibrary loans and renewals. Further examples of processes are provided in the toolkit. In the criterion, mention is also made of value-added processes, ie procedures which add value to the services that the customers receive.

The process criterion was derived from the examples set out in the Business Excellence Model (BQF, 1997). Two key areas of process management were identified:

- **Processes (6a)** How are processes managed?
- **Processes (6b)** How are processes improved?

To address this criterion the assessment team must consider how processes are planned, developed, implemented and improved across the whole library and information service.

PROCESSES (6A) HOW ARE PROCESSES MANAGED?

Here, the assessment team is required to assess how key processes are managed in the library and information service. This includes addressing what mechanisms are in place to support their identification, planning and implementation. Other issues to address include how working practices and procedures are documented and aligned across the service. Again, best-practice organizations will also be able to provide evidence of meaningful performance targets and objectives for key processes.

PROCESSES (6B) HOW ARE PROCESSES IMPROVED?

Evidence is required for how working practices and procedures are improved to maximize their effectiveness. There are clear links between this sub-criterion and (4d) employee involvement. Evidence should show that strategies to support employee involvement in process improvement are in place. Other critical issues include the role that benchmarking plays in process improvement.

LINKS TO OTHER CRITERIA

The management and development of processes is also addressed in sub-criteria (2a), (3a) and (4a).

EXAMPLES OF GOOD PRACTICE

- The use of process-mapping techniques to identify and address key bottlenecks.
- The improvement and assessment of processes by benchmarking against best-practice organizations.
- The use of quality standards and systems such as ISO 9000 to define and document key working practices and procedures to document working procedures.

Customer satisfaction

In recent years measures of customer satisfaction with library and information services such as MORI polls or Audit Commission indicators, have received significant criticism because they do little to challenge the traditional notion of what these services can achieve (Usherwood, 1998). Similarly, there is a suggestion that customers have generally low expectations of library and information services (Aslib, 1995). Discussions with the demonstrator authorities showed that there was a real desire to identify sophisticated approaches to assess customer satisfaction, through, for example, focus groups. Indeed, library services A and C were already involved in this type of activity. A critical issue in self-assessment is the identification of links between what is planned and what is achieved, and therefore the library and information service should be able to identify why particular satisfaction measures are being used and implemented.

The indicators of customer satisfaction were derived from the Business Excellence Model (BQF, 1997). However, discussion with the demonstrator authorities suggested that the way in which satisfaction was measured also required development. To this end three sub-criteria were identified:

- **Customer satisfaction (7a)** How is customer satisfaction managed?
- **Customer satisfaction (7b)** How is customer satisfaction measured?
- **Customer satisfaction (7c)** What are the results in customer satisfaction?

How the library service plans, develops, implements and reviews methods to identify customer satisfaction, its measures of satisfaction, and the results in customer satisfaction should be addressed.

CUSTOMER SATISFACTION (7A) HOW IS CUSTOMER SATISFACTION MANAGED?

The assessment team requires evidence of the methods used to identify customer satisfaction and how they are assessed for effectiveness. It is critical to address the processes for identifying appropriate methods to assess customer satisfaction; best-practice organizations will use methods to identify both management data and customer perceptions. Methods of identifying customer perceptions will also include more experimental techniques such as customer forums and comments and complaints procedures. Again, best-practice organizations will ensure that the methods are assessed for their effectiveness, ie that they are appropriate techniques to identify the indicators discussed under sub-criterion (7b).

CUSTOMER SATISFACTION (7B) HOW IS CUSTOMER SATISFACTION MEASURED?

Here the assessment team is looking for evidence relating to the measures or indicators of customer satisfaction and how the library and information service assesses them for relevance. Both management indicators of customer satisfaction and evidence relating to customer perception of satisfaction should be identified. However, the critical issue to address is how the library and information service plans, develops and implements relevant measures of customer satisfaction. Evidence should also show that these measures are aligned to the organization's overall plans, policies and strategies and that they are regularly reviewed for their effectiveness. Performance targets, objectives and benchmarks for customer satisfaction should also be assessed for their relevance and effectiveness.

CUSTOMER SATISFACTION (7C) WHAT ARE THE RESULTS IN CUSTOMER SATISFACTION?

Here, the assessment team is assessing the results, trends and targets the library and information service achieves in customer satisfaction and how these relate to best-practice organizations. The results may be qualitative or quantitative, but the evidence should show that they are continuously improving.

LINKS TO OTHER CRITERIA

Issues relating to customer satisfaction are also dealt with in sub-criterion (3c).

EXAMPLES OF GOOD PRACTICE

- Internal indicators such as stock turnover and membership levels.
- Identifying degree of satisfaction with service – reliability, choice, accessibility.
- Identifying degree of satisfaction with staff – courtesy, availability, knowledge, performance.
- Identifying perceptions on value for money.
- Identifying perceptions on equity in treatment.
- Identifying perceptions on user education.
- Identifying perceptions on equipment and buildings.
- Ensuring that all indicators are benchmarked, targets set and trends analysed.
- Ensuring that all indicators are derived from planned activities.

Employee satisfaction

The rhetoric of employee empowerment and development has pervaded recent library management literature (Boelke, 1995; Milner, Kinnell and

Usherwood, 1995). While many library and information services are involved in staff training and development (Oldroyd, 1996; Milner, Kinnell and Usherwood, 1997) the literature has little evidence of formal mechanisms to assess employee satisfaction outside appraisal schemes. However, in recent surveys a significant percentage of public-library authorities and academic libraries were implementing staff appraisal (Milner, Kinnell and Usherwood, 1997; Garrod and Kinnell, 1997). Two of the demonstrator services had yet to implement any direct employee satisfaction survey. Jordan and Jones (1995) identified a number of staff motivators and demotivators that might be used to assess employee satisfaction.

Discussions with the demonstrator authorities showed that there was a desire to take forward the rhetoric of employee satisfaction and to implement real mechanisms which could identify results and lead to an increase in employee satisfaction. A critical issue in self-assessment is the identification of links between what is planned and what is achieved. Therefore measures of employee satisfaction should be linked to planned activities.

The indicators of employee satisfaction were derived from the Business Excellence Model (BQF, 1997). To this end three sub-criteria were identified:

- **Employee satisfaction (8a)** How is employee satisfaction managed?
- **Employee satisfaction (8b)** How is employee satisfaction measured?
- **Employee satisfaction (8c)** What are the results in employee satisfaction?

How the library and information service plans, develops, implements and reviews methods to identify employee satisfaction, measures of satisfaction, and the results in employee satisfaction should be addressed.

EMPLOYEE SATISFACTION (8A) HOW IS EMPLOYEE SATISFACTION MANAGED?

The assessment team requires evidence of the methods used to identify employee satisfaction and how they are assessed for effectiveness. It is critical to address the processes for identifying appropriate methods to assess employee satisfaction; best-practice organizations will use methods to identify both management data and employee perceptions. Methods of identifying employee perceptions will also include more experimental techniques such as employee forums and comments and complaints procedures. Again, best-practice organizations will ensure that the methods are assessed for their effectiveness, ie that they are appropriate techniques to identify the indicators discussed under sub-criterion (8b).

EMPLOYEE SATISFACTION (8B) HOW IS EMPLOYEE SATISFACTION MEASURED?

Here the assessment team is looking for evidence relating to the measures or indicators of employee satisfaction and how the library and information service assesses them for relevance. Both management indicators of employee satisfaction and evidence relating to employee perception of job satisfaction should be identified. However, the critical issue to address is how the library and information service plans, develops and implements relevant measures of employee satisfaction. Evidence should also show that these measures are aligned to the organization's overall plans, policies and strategies and that they are regularly reviewed for their effectiveness. Performance targets, objectives and benchmarks for employee satisfaction should also be assessed for their relevance and effectiveness.

EMPLOYEE SATISFACTION (8C) WHAT ARE THE RESULTS IN EMPLOYEE SATISFACTION?

Here, the assessment team is assessing the results, trends and targets the library and information service achieves in employee satisfaction and how these relate to best-practice organizations. The results may be qualitative or quantitative, but the evidence should show that they are continuously improving.

EXAMPLES OF GOOD PRACTICE

- Internal indicators such as sick leave, turnover of staff, absenteeism.
- Perceptions on motivation, eg empowerment, involvement, career development, recognition, leadership, equality of opportunity.

- Using organizational health checks, exit interviews and appraisal to identify employee satisfaction.
- Perceptions on working conditions, eg equipment, terms and conditions, job security, management of change.
- Ensuring that all indicators are benchmarked, targets set and trends analysed.
- Ensuring that all indicators are derived from planned activities.

Impact on society

In theory library and information services can have an impact in many areas, such as literacy, citizenship and educational achievement. However, until recently there has been a dearth of mechanisms to demonstrate this (Matarasso, 1998). Within the past few years there has been a growing trend to identify meaningful indicators of the value and impact of library and information services (Linley and Usherwood, 1998). This criterion offers library and information service managers a useful political tool for use with resource providers and senior managers. A critical issue in self-assessment is the identification of links between what is planned and what is achieved. Therefore measures of impact on society should be linked to planned activities. Some library and information services, particularly public library services, will find this criterion easier to deal with than others; however, knowing and understanding how the service impacts on all stakeholders will provide useful evidence for the planning of services.

The indicators of impact on society were derived from work undertaken on the impact of public library services (Linley and Usherwood, 1998; Matarraso, 1998). To this end three sub-criteria were identified:

- **Impact on society (9a)** How is impact on society managed?
- **Impact on society (9b)** How is impact on society measured?
- **Impact on society (9c)** What are the results in impact on society?

How the library and information service plans, develops, implements and reviews methods to identify impact on society, measures of satisfaction, and the results in impact on society should be addressed.

IMPACT ON SOCIETY (9A) HOW IS IMPACT ON SOCIETY MANAGED?

The assessment team requires evidence of the methods used to identify impact on society and how they are assessed for effectiveness. It is critical to address the processes for identifying appropriate methods to assess impact on society; best-practice organizations will use methods to identify both management data and customer perceptions. Methods of identifying customer perceptions will also include more experimental techniques such as customer forums and comments and complaints procedures. Again, best-practice organizations will ensure that the methods are assessed for their effectiveness, ie that there are appropriate techniques to identify the indicators discussed under sub-criterion (9b).

IMPACT ON SOCIETY (9B) HOW IS IMPACT ON SOCIETY MEASURED?

Here the assessment team is looking for evidence relating to the measures or indicators of impact on society and how the library and information service assesses them for relevance. Both management indicators of impact on society satisfaction and evidence relating to society's perception of impact should be identified. However, the critical issue to address is how the library and information service plans, develops and implements relevant measures of the impact on society - how it evaluates and understands its impact on society. Evidence should also show that these measures are aligned to the organization's overall plans, policies and strategies and that they are regularly reviewed for their effectiveness. Performance targets, objectives and benchmarks for the impact on society should also be assessed for their relevance and effectiveness.

IMPACT ON SOCIETY (9C) WHAT ARE THE RESULTS IN IMPACT ON SOCIETY?

Here, the assessment team is assessing the results, trends and targets the library and information service achieves in its impact on society and how these relate to best-practice organizations. The results may be qualitative or quantitative, but the evidence should show that they are continuously improving.

EXAMPLES OF GOOD PRACTICE

- Internal indicators such as the number of voluntary/community groups linked to the service, contacts with outside organizations, and numbers accessing training programmes/facilities (Matarasso, 1998).
- Undertaking a social audit to identify the perceptions and attitudes of key stakeholders.
- Identifying perceptions of social impact.
- Identifying perceptions of economic impact.
- Identifying perceptions of impact on equity.
- Ensuring that all indicators are benchmarked, targets set and trends analysed.
- Ensuring that all indicators are derived from planned activities.

Overall performance

A critical issue in self-assessment is the identification of links between what is planned and what is achieved.

The indicators of overall performance were derived from the Business Excellence Model (BQF, 1997). To this end three sub-criteria were identified:

- **Overall performance (10a)** How is overall performance managed?
- **Overall performance (10b)** How is overall performance measured?
- **Overall performance (10c)** What are the results in overall performance?

How the library and information service plans, develops, implements and reviews methods to identify overall performance, measures of satisfaction, and the results in overall performance should be addressed.

OVERALL PERFORMANCE (10A) HOW IS OVERALL PERFORMANCE MANAGED?

The assessment team requires evidence of the methods used to identify overall performance and how they are assessed for effectiveness. It is critical to address the processes for identifying appropriate methods to assess overall performance; best-practice organizations will use methods to identify both management data and customer perceptions. Methods of identifying customer perceptions will also include more experimental techniques such as customer forums and comments and complaints procedures. Again, best-practice organizations will ensure that the methods are assessed for their effectiveness, ie that there are appropriate techniques to identify the indicators discussed under sub-criterion (10b).

OVERALL PERFORMANCE (10B) HOW IS OVERALL PERFORMANCE MEASURED?

Here, the assessment team is looking for evidence relating to the measures or indicators of overall performance and how the library and information service assesses them for relevance. The critical issue to address is how the library and information service plans, develops and implements relevant measures of overall performance. Evidence should also show that these measures are aligned to the organization's overall plans, policies and strategies and that they are regularly reviewed for their effectiveness. Performance targets, objectives and benchmarks for overall performance should also be assessed for their relevance and effectiveness.

OVERALL PERFORMANCE (10C) WHAT ARE THE RESULTS IN OVERALL PERFORMANCE?

Here, the assessment team is assessing the results, trends and targets the library and information service achieves in overall performance and how these relate to best-practice organizations. The results may be qualitative or quantitative, but the evidence should show that they are continuously improving.

EXAMPLES OF GOOD PRACTICE

- Internal indicators such as financial results (eg year-on-year efficiency gains), achievement of policy and strategy, efficiency and effectiveness measures - resources, technology, information, response rates, complaints handling, stock turnover, process improvements, Audit Commission performance indicators.

- Ensuring that all indicators are benchmarked, targets set and trends analysed.
- Ensuring that all indicators are derived from planned activities.

Summary and conclusion

The criteria listed here form the basis of the self-assessment process. The library and information service will be assessed against them. Further examples of appropriate evidence are provided with the criteria in Section 4 of the resource pack. Library and information managers should ensure that the types of issues that they are asked to address are relevant to the service. Some issues will be more relevant than others. However, the criteria do provide a structured framework for identifying improvement opportunities.

The LISIM was developed through a process of iteration and trial in the demonstrator services. The model was designed to support planning processes and the delivery and review of effective services. By including elements from all three of the theoretical models that were the focus of the study it provides a tailored approach to self-assessment to meet the needs of public sector information organizations. Critically, it includes consideration of the library and information services' customer focus and impacts on society, and of the local authority or other public sector context in which the services are being delivered. The next chapter provides detailed guidelines for library and information managers who are planning self-assessment.

References

Aslib (1995) *Review of the public library service in England and Wales for the Department of National Heritage: final report*, Aslib.

Barnard, S B (1993) Implementing total quality management: a model for research libraries. In Jurow, S and Barnard S B (eds) *Integrating total quality management in a library setting*, The Haworth Press.

Boelke, J H (1995) *Quality improvement in libraries: total quality management and related approaches*, Advances in Librarianship 19, Academic Press.

BQF (1997) *Guide to self-assessment: public sector guidelines*, British Quality Foundation.

Brophy, P and Coulling, K (1997) Quality management in libraries. In Brockman, J (ed) *Quality management and benchmarking in the information sector*, Bowker-Saur.

Foley, E G (1994) *Winning European quality*, European Foundation for Quality Management.

Frank, R C (1993) Total quality management: the Federal Government experience. In Jurow, S and Barnard, S B (eds) *Integrating total quality management in a library setting*, The Haworth Press.

Garrod, P and Kinnell, M (1997) Towards library excellence: best practice benchmarking in the library and information sector. In Brockman, J (ed) *Quality management and benchmarking in the information sector*, Bowker-Saur.

Goulding, A, Mistry, S, Proctor, R and Kinnell, M (1999) *Investing in LIS people: the impact of the IiP initiative on the library and information centre*, BLRIC. (Forthcoming)

Jones, K, Kinnell, M and Usherwood, B (1999) The development of self-assessment tool-kits for the library and information sector, *Journal of Documentation*. (Forthcoming)

Jones, K, Kinnell, M and Usherwood, B (1999) *Planning for public library improvement: Report of the second project workshop*, Department of Information Science, Loughborough University.

Jordan, P and Jones, N (1995) *Staff management in library and information work*, 3rd edn, Gower.

Jurow, S and Barnard, S B (eds) (1993) *Integrating total quality management in a library setting*, The Haworth Press.

LGMB (1997) *Quality initiatives: report of the findings from the 1997 survey of local authority activity*, Local Government Management Board.

Linley, R and Usherwood, B (1998) *New measures for the new library: a social audit of public libraries. British Library Research and Innovation Centre Report 89*, Department of Information Studies, University of Sheffield.

Matarasso, F (1998) *Beyond book issues: the social potential of library projects*, Comedia.

Miller R G and Stearns, B (1994) Quality management for today's academic library, *College and Research Libraries News*, **48**, 110-22.

Milner, E, Kinnell, M and Usherwood, B (1995) Employee suggestion schemes: a management tool for the 1990s, *Library Management*, **16** (3), 3-8.

Milner, E, Kinnell, M and Usherwood, B (1997) Quality management and public library services. In Brockman, J (ed) *Quality management and benchmarking in the information sector*, Bowker-Saur.

Oldroyd, M (ed) (1996) *Staff development in academic libraries: present practice and future challenges*, Library Association Publishing.

Pfeffer, N and Coote, A (1991) *Is quality good for you?*, Institute of Public Policy Research.

St Clair, G (1994) *Power and influence: enhancing information services within the organisation*, Bowker-Saur.

Sirkin, A F (1993) Customer service: another side of TQM. In Jurow, S and Barnard, S B (eds) *Integrating total quality management in a library setting*, The Haworth Press.

Spiller, D (ed) (1998) *Public library plans. Proceedings of a seminar held at Loughborough University 17-18 March 1998*, LISU.

Stewart, J and Walsh, K (1989) *The search for quality*, Local Government Training Board.

Usherwood, B (1998) Much more than numbers, *The Bookseller*, (8 May), 28-9.

Weingand, D E (1997) *Customer service excellence: a concise guide for librarians*, American Library Association.

5
Undertaking self-assessment

Introduction

A successful self-assessment is very much dependent upon the library and information service having appropriate strategies in place to manage the process effectively. This involves a great deal of planning and preparation on the part of the lead officer to ensure that the assessment runs smoothly. Once awareness is raised and support for assessment gained across the service, the assessment model must be identified and training programmes implemented. The actual assessment is then undertaken, scoring takes place and consensus about improvement activities is gained. The process concludes with the delivery of post-assessment improvement plans. This chapter examines the issues which should be addressed when implementing self-assessment. The discussion is illustrated with examples of how three public library services undertook self-assessment, and outlines the critical success factors for its efficient and effective implementation.

Implementing self-assessment in library and information services

Effective leadership is crucial to enable self-assessment to be implemented successfully within library and information services. The managers of the process will have a key role to play in developing a self-assessment framework for their organizations. They will be responsible for all stages of the process, from raising initial awareness to the delivery of post-assessment improvement plans and reports (Conti, 1997).

The library and information manager must first determine how self-assessment should be incorporated into the management framework of the organization. The approach taken will have a significant impact on how far the initiative becomes embedded into the culture of the service. The manager must decide whether self-assessment should be undertaken as an organization-wide enterprise or whether individual units or departments should be encouraged to identify and implement their own approach (Hakes, 1994).

The decision on how to implement self-assessment presents a dilemma to the library and information manager, the resolution of which will determine how self-assessment is perceived, understood and managed throughout the entire service. The choice of approach needs careful consideration, since it will impact on staff understanding of the process and their desire to take part in the enterprise. If self-assessment is executed as an organization-wide approach, then it is likely that a broad ownership of the operation will be established. However, this will depend very much on how far those championing self-assessment are involved in the day-to-day management of the service.

With separate units developing their own process, middle managers will generally be considered its key champions and the organization will depend on their understanding, cooperation and support. Indeed, Van der Wiele et al suggest (1995, 93) that 'it is important that managers take the initiative of applying self-assessment to their own area of responsibility'. How far self-assessment is accepted by all staff will be influenced by whether the process is perceived to constitute a threat or an opportunity to the normal working routine of the library and information service. Staff who are involved in the process and who have developed a sense of ownership are more likely to be open to change, and therefore less likely to perceive it as a threat.

Initial considerations

During the lead-up to self-assessment, each of the demonstrator services was asked to consider a number of questions about how they wished to manage the process, based in part on the pre-assessment checklist identified by Hakes (1994, 191-8). These questions aimed to provide an opportunity for the organizations to identify and plan how their self-assessment would be approached. Other managerial and administrative issues were raised during the course of the self-assessment, and these also needed to be addressed. This section takes each of these points in turn, and identifies the types of questions which need to be considered and why they are important. Where relevant, the discussion is illustrated by drawing on the example of the demonstrator services.

Identifying the role of self-assessment

At the beginning of the process, the organization should endeavour to identify the role or purpose of self-assessment (Jones, Kinnell and Usherwood, 1998a). This provides a basis for the planning, communication and administration of the exercise, and shows an understanding on the part of management that there will be issues raised by the self-assessment that will require attention. It also suggests that there is a commitment and determination to improve the service at a senior level.

Part of the discussion here has been covered in more detail in Chapter 3. However, in the context of this discussion it is worth recapitulating why self-assessment might be considered:

- to review the management practices of the service
- to provide a focus for implementing total quality in the service
- to identify what the service is achieving against models of best practice.

By articulating the role of self-assessment within the library and information service, the manager will have a base from which to determine the aims, objectives and critical success factors of the process. Clearly stated aims and objectives facilitate the efficient and effective communication and promotion of self-assessment across the organization by outlining what the service wants to achieve, how it will achieve it and what the expected outcomes of the process will be. The critical success factors also provide the grounds for determining the value and impact of self-assessment on the service in the post-assessment review. If the role cannot be formulated, then the manager must consider whether the process will be worthwhile. In a survey of European organizations undertaking self-assessment, Van der Wiele et al (1996, 59-60) expressed concern that lead officers did not always consider this question:

> Many respondents had problems defining the goals and acheivements for self-assessment. This is a serious problem . . . other managers and employees will be even less aware of the reasons and goals underlying self-assessment.

Knowing why self-assessment is needed provides the basis for informing others of the decision to undertake self-assessment, and enables one to gain the commitment of the key participants in the process.

Managing the self-assessment process

Stage one: Committing to the process

The route to self-assessment begins with the initial decision to commit to the process (Holloway, 1995; Jones, Kinnell and Usherwood, 1998a). This decision cannot be properly taken without those who are to be involved in the assessment being fully informed of their duties and responsibilities in carrying out the task. Any library and information service considering self-assessment needs to be aware that such an undertaking requires:

- the involvement and consent of key staff to ensure that the exercise runs smoothly
- the cooperation of all staff to maximize the potential benefits to the service
- the necessary resources to implement self-assessment
- the motivation to undertake post-assessment improvements.

Within the organization, staff will have differing degrees of involvement and participation in the self-assessment process:

- Senior managers will have an important role to play in encouraging participation and promoting the value of self-assessment across the

service. They will also be responsible for ensuring that the lead managers have the authority and power to facilitate the process effectively.
- The professional managing the assessment will be charged with ensuring that it meets its aims and objectives and that it is undertaken efficiently and effectively.
- The members of the assessment team will be responsible for making sure that they undertake a fair and impartial critique of the current management practices within the service.
- Those staff who are not directly involved in the project will have a role in cooperating with the assessment team, ensuring that all relevant evidence is made available.

The task of gaining senior management commitment to undertake self-assessment involves helping them to identify the value and potential of the process for the service. They will need to be informed as to what self-assessment is and how it can add value to the performance-measurement activities already undertaken by the service. Showing that the process is being increasingly adopted across the public sector, and that there is a growing interest within the library and information sector in its potential as a planning tool, will undoubtedly help foster their interest. Self-assessment can also have the added value of educating senior managers about the role of quality in organizations; models of good practice are 'a useful tool to grab senior managers' attention, and help them to begin to appreciate quality as a much broader concept than merely a series of standards' (Wright, 1997, 320). Session 1 of Section 2 of the training pack provides further evidence for its value. Senior managers will also need to be made aware of the costs of the process, such as staff time and the extra administrative costs. Ideally, one senior manager should agree to champion the process within the service. This senior manager will be responsible for providing input and support to the evaluation, and ensuring the team has the necessary tools to undertake the assessment. Crucially, this manager must also show a commitment to act on the results of the assessment. It is recommended that this manager should undertake a suitable training programme. 'Commitment and involvement from the top is essential in this situation if the whole process is to be successful in generating sustainable results'. (Black and Crumbley, 1997, 91)

While library service C was keen to undertake self-assessment, a lack of key personnel at senior management level meant that the decision was taken to put the assessment on hold. Given the number of organizations that have testified that senior management commitment is vital to the successful implementation of self-assessment (Van der Wiele et al, 1996), the decision to postpone can be seen as an appropriate course of action.

Gaining the commitment of those staff who will be involved in undertaking the self-assessment will depend on how they have been selected to participate. The decision of who to involve is discussed in further detail below. Those who are willing to take part because they are interested in learning more about the process will already have a degree of commitment to the exercise. If, however, they have been instructed to take part, then first they need to be informed about what self-assessment involves and how it can add value to their own role within the service.

Approaches to inform those staff who will not be directly involved in the process also need to be developed. They are likely to be aware that some kind of assessment is being undertaken, and may be concerned about its impact on their day-to-day routines, particularly if these are changed as a result of the assessment. Here, it is not necessary to give detailed accounts of the self-assessment process, rather the emphasis should be on the outcomes of the process, ie how the results of the assessment might bring improvements to working practices across the library service. Again, Session 1 of the resource pack provides guidelines on how to facilitate this.

As with any new initiative, staff can often be sceptical about the value of self-assessment, and may see it as an added burden to their normal routine. This issue is a common phenomenon in the development of quality management programmes (Jurow and Barnard, 1993; Milner, Kinnell and Usherwood, 1997), and requires careful mediation to ensure that it does not hinder the process. If staff cannot identify with the potential of self-assessment or regard it as the latest management fad, then they are unlikely to offer full support and the attention to detail which is required in the process. As one librarian suggested in discussion:

> For any kind of quality initiative they've [staff] got to see it's going to improve lives – customers' lives, staff lives – you've got to be able to show them a concrete reason for it.

The library and information service manager must identify mechanisms for dealing with cynicism.

Staff involvement is fundamental to maintaining the impetus in self-assessment. This process begins by involving staff at all stages in the development of the initiative, and by having mechanisms in place to achieve ownership. The demonstrator services used the following mechanisms to raise awareness of, and encourage participation in, the self-assessment:

- In two of the demonstrator services regular meetings were held with an external facilitator to share concerns and answer queries.
- Newsletters were used in all three services as a way of informing all staff about the self-assessment process. A timetable was provided alongside an explanation of the process and a series of key questions and answers.
- One service provided elected members and its senior management team with regular minutes and memos to outline the process and its potential impact on the library service.
- One demonstrator service held a workshop to explore in detail issues surrounding employee management, one of the key assessment criteria in the LISIM. This enabled the service to show the relevance of self-assessment by focusing on one area where improvements would impact on all staff.
- Training was provided in the services which undertook the actual self-assessment. The training programme is discussed in more detail later in this chapter.

IDENTIFYING THE SELF-ASSESSMENT TEAM

A key question which the library and information service must consider is which members of staff will be involved in undertaking the self-assessment. There are four clear issues to be addressed here:

- Who will have responsibility for administering the self-assessment?
- Which employees will be involved in the self-assessment?
- What section of the service will these employees be drawn from?
- What roles will individual team members undertake?

The choice of lead officer will have a significant influence on the outcome of the self-assessment. As the senior team member, this manager will be responsible for ensuring that the process is completed as efficiently and comprehensively as possible. The manager must also ensure that team members receive sufficient support and assistance as they undertake the assessment. Therefore, the library and information service must provide the assessment team with the necessary authority to undertake the evaluation, ie all staff should be made aware that they are expected to cooperate fully with the team. In order to lead the process effectively, the lead manager should receive appropriate training on undertaking the process, and adequate guidelines on the timing, aims and objectives of the assessment. While many of the decisions about the actual assessment might not be taken until after the team is formed, it is important that the lead officer is provided with an adequate framework within which to make these decisions.

The two public library services which piloted the assessment process appointed a range of staff to the role of lead officer:

- The lead manager in library service A had been involved in establishing their original quality programme and was now responsible for maintaining and developing the quality policy across the service.
- Library service B took a team approach, with various members of staff leading on different aspects of the programme.

Careful consideration will also need to be given to the question of who should be included on the assessment team (Conti, 1997). While it is possible for one person to undertake the entire assessment, it is perhaps more effective to take a team approach. Ideally, the team should contain between five and eight staff members, but this will obviously depend on the size of the library and information service. Using a team approach will provide a more even-handed view of what the service is achieving, although this will depend on which sections of the service the team members are drawn from. As Table 5.1 shows, one-person assessments can lead to unquestioned bias and misguided assumptions about aspects of the service which the assessor is not aware of, or does not fully understand. Consequently, the professional involved may have difficulty in persuading staff that the results validly reflect current practice.

Table 5.1   *Advantages and disadvantages of different approaches to self-assessment*

one-person assessment	senior-manager assessment
Advantages	**Advantages**
• working within own timetable	• senior managers have broad understanding of the whole service
• working within own frame of reference	
Disadvantages	**Disadvantages**
• unquestioned assumptions/bias	• may be seen as just another management fad
• results may not be accepted by all staff	• senior managers may not be willing to share poor results

front-line assessment	mixed-team assessment
Advantages	**Advantages**
• opinions of those who are often ignored in decision-making process gained	• range of opinions gained offer a more balanced view of service achievements
• staff development opportunity	• wider staff ownership of results because all areas of the service are represented
Disadvantages	**Disadvantages**
• front-line staff may not have sufficient understanding of all relevant issues	• difficulty in working within fixed timetable
• areas for improvement may have an operational bias	• difficult to gain a consensus about important issues to address

When considering the composition of the team, it is worth attempting to gain as broad a coverage as possible, in order to avoid guesswork or unwarranted assumptions. In smaller library and information services which may only have one permanent member of staff, it might be worthwhile inviting an external assessor to join the team, either to help undertake the assessment or to act as a source of external validation. This external assessor may be drawn from within the same organization, or from a similar service which has experience of self-assessment.

The assessment team in library service A was drawn from staff who were involved in establishing and taking forward the original quality programme. The majority of team members who were appointed held supervisory positions, ranging from middle to senior managers. All aspects of the service were represented on the team, although to avoid having too many participants, where input was needed for only one or two sub-criteria, relevant experts were called upon as and when required.

Library service B employed a smaller assessment team to manage the process. Again, they had been involved in the development of the original drive for quality. The assessment team was again drawn from those staff with supervisory experience. However, the actual assessment was undertaken by a number of teams, each representing their own section of the service.

The roles attributed to individual team members will depend upon the dynamics of the group, and each option has its own advantages and disadvantages. These are discussed later in this chapter.

Stage two: The model/approach

CHOOSING THE SELF-ASSESSMENT MODEL/APPROACH

Self-assessment takes place against a model of good management practice. This can either be a generic model developed to suit a wide range of organizations, or a specific management model developed with one particular type of organization in mind. Any library and information service wishing to undertake a self-assessment must first decide whether to use a generic or a specific model.

There are a number of issues which the manager must consider when choosing a model for assessment purposes:

- whether the library and information service aspires to meet the demands of the inherent principles or the underlying management ethos of the model
- whether the model is easy to interpret and understand
- what costs are involved in developing and using the model
- what training is required to use the model
- what self-assessment methods the model supports.

Table 5.2 *Differences between tailored and generic models of good management practice*

generic approach	tailored approach
Advantages	**Advantages**
• facilitates benchmarking across public sector and private sector	• sector-specific
• facilitates discussion across public sector and private sector	• tailored to operational context
• potentially higher usage levels	• facilitates benchmarking within the library and information sector
Disadvantages	**Disadvantages**
• may have to change language to suit organization	• benchmarking outside of the library and information sector may be problematic
• areas to address and criteria may not be fully relevant	• self-assessment of departments within wider organizational context (eg local authority/university) will not be within the same terms of reference

Once the assessment model has been chosen, it is then necessary for the library and information service to decide whether or not to tailor the approach (see Table 5.2). Again, research has shown that those public sector organizations with experience of using good practice models have tended to change them to suit their own culture, experience and level of quality maturity (Reed, 1997). Some organizations, such as the Further Education Funding Council, have developed specific self-assessment guidelines for colleges of FE (FEFC, 1997). Other organizations such as the Benefits Agency have merely simplified the language of existing models in order to make them more 'user-friendly' for staff (Whitford and Bird, 1996).

This value-added approach, ie tailoring and adapting the approach, can be time consuming, but will ultimately have a beneficial impact on the organization, simply because the approach will be made directly relevant to all those who will be involved in undertaking the assessment. Adapting the model to the organization can help strengthen the impact of the approach and ensure that it becomes an 'effective planning and self-assessment tool' (Conti, 1997, 111). If the decision is taken to tailor the approach, then there are two issues which must be addressed:

- whether to tailor the content of the model by changing or removing assessment criteria

- whether to change the language of the model to support wider interpretation and understanding.

Reed (1995, 11) identified nine criteria to help organizations decide how appropriate the self-assessment model and approach was:

- culture and style of the organization - the current management approaches and assessment styles the organization implements
- level of resources available - what resources are required to support the assessment process
- objectives of the organization - what the organization wishes to achieve from the self-assessment
- level of TQM understanding within the organization
- time available for the actual assessment
- potential threats, as perceived by staff
- potential benefits as perceived by staff
- size of organization to be assessed
- geographical dispersal of the organization.

The LISIM supplied in the toolkit was developed using input from a number of practitioners. As a consequence it is unlikely to need to be tailored for content. However, some of the examples provided of relevant initiatives may require some modification. The decision as to whether or not to tailor the approach will depend on who will be involved in the actual assessment. The language of the model was chosen to reflect the experience of staff in management positions within library and information services, and as a consequence staff in front-line positions may not always understand the concepts and terminology used.

Table 5.3 (page 112) summarizes a variety of methods which might be employed in self-assessment. The training pack provides comprehensive guidelines on how to implement the pro-forma approach within a workshop setting. While other organizations have tried different methods to facilitate their self-assessment, comments from one demonstrator service and the literature suggest that the pro-forma offers a more complete assessment, and provides a simple and flexible approach to the actual process. Other advantages include the ability to identify strengths, weaknesses and key areas for improvement (BQF, 1997). The questions asked in the pro-forma were informed by the literature (Stewart and Walsh, 1989; Pfeffer and Coote, 1991; BQF, 1997; Hakes, 1994) and by discussions with the demonstrator authorities. For example, library service A suggested the need to ask how consistently approaches were adhered to, because 'we need to identify what we don't do'.

The toolkit provides three methods for undertaking self-assessment, each offering different levels of thoroughness and accuracy:

- The LISIM presents a matrix approach to self-assessment; the library and information service can match its current position on the matrix and identify where it fits against good practice.
- The simple questionnaire shown in Session 5 gives a very quick and simple example of self-assessment and can be used for awareness raising and to facilitate discussion across the service.
- The pro-forma offers a comprehensive self-assessment, including a robust scoring mechanism and the ability to identify future improvement actions.

Some organizations such as the Post Office have opted for this 'tiered approach to self-assessment, utilising methods appropriately modified for different levels of the organisation' (Black and Crumbley, 1997, 91)

PILOTING SELF-ASSESSMENT

As with any new initiative, it must be decided whether or not to pilot the process before employing it across the whole library and information service (Hakes, 1994). Piloting self-assessment will enable the team to test the reliability and validity of the approach they have decided to adopt. It will enable the lead officer to identify shortfalls in expectations and examine what areas might require further attention.

Piloting self-assessment will be particularly useful for those library and information sector organizations which decide to tailor or adapt in-house an existing model of good practice. Without piloting, untested models and approaches may come unstuck during the self-assessment, and it will be difficult to rectify this once the exercise has begun. The consequences of this can be critical, particularly in terms of the commitment of the lead officers involved.

Table 5.3   *Advantages and disadvantages of self-assessment methods (TQMI, 1997; BQF, 1997)*

self-assessment approach	interviews	matrix	peer assess-ment	pro-forma	question-naire	workshop
advantages:						
awareness raising		•	•	•	•	•
benchmarking		•	•		•	
cross function learning	•	•		•	•	•
easily customised	•	•		•	•	•
facilitates discussion	•	•	•	•	•	•
identifies current position	•	•	•	•	•	•
identifies strengths	•		•	•		•
identifies weaknesses	•		•	•		•
involves senior management		•	•	•	•	
potentially wide use		•			•	•
robust scoring			•	•	•	
simple approach		•			•	
team building				•		•
training tool				•		•
disadvantages:						
addresses 'what' not 'why'		•			•	
data analysis can overwhelm	•			•	•	•
have to identify approach	•		•		•	
low response rate					•	
narrow use		•				
no benchmarking						
no identification of strengths		•			•	
no identification of weaknesses		•			•	
not scored to full specification	•	•				
progression unclear	•				•	•
provides a summary of position		•		•	•	
requires careful planning	•		•	•	•	
requires facilitation		•	•	•		•
requires management time	•		•	•		•
resource intensive	•		•	•	•	•
staff intensive	•		•	•	•	•
time intensive	•		•	•	•	•

In particular there are a number of key issues which the manager must try and address when assessing the pilot:

- Did staff understand the language and terminology used in the approach?
- Did staff understand the actual process of undertaking self-assessment?
- What critical issues arose during the process which required immediate handling?

The lead manager will also be able to use the pilot as a means of identifying what practical issues involved in planning the assessment are likely to require attention, such as how many people to involve, what constitutes evidence, and how easily consensus is reached. The results from the pilot can then be used as a basis for monitoring and validating the results from the entire organization.

If the library and information service is unable to pilot self-assessment due to limitations in time or resources, then Sessions 4 and 5 in the training pack will give those undertaking the assessment the opportunity to undertake a dry run of the process before the full exercise is carried out.

While none of the demonstrator authorities piloted self-assessment within their library service, they did in effect act as pilot authorities for the self-assessment model and criteria outlined in Chapter 4. Feedback from library and information professionals led to various improvements and alterations to the final model. It also provided the basis for much of the discussion of the intricacies of self-assessment which have been outlined in this chapter.

IDENTIFYING THE OUTCOME OF SELF-ASSESSMENT

One critical issue which must be addressed before the assessment is undertaken is what form of outcome the assessment should produce. There are a number of options available to the library and information service manager:

- identifying the services' current standing against a model of good practice
- identifying strengths and weaknesses in current management practices

- identifying a self-assessment score.

Knowing where the service fits against a model of good practice can provide the manager with a clear idea of those areas which may require attention in a full self-assessment. This is a very simple form of self-assessment, but it does give a realistic summary of what gaps there are in current service planning. This method is useful for those organizations deciding whether or not to commit to the full-scale approach or those undertaking self-assessment for the first time. It can also be useful for senior management teams which may not have time to undertake the full assessment.

To identify strengths and weaknesses against a model of good practice can be very time-consuming, yet in terms of outcome this approach is perhaps the most useful for library and information services since it facilitates detailed service planning. However, the service must be prepared to deal with the issues that are raised as a result of the assessment.

The majority of self-assessment methods outlined in the previous section lend themselves to the identification of a score. In the case of the LISM, progress against each criterion is scored out of 100, leading to a total score between 0 and 1000.

When assessing its planning processes, the library service will be seeking to score its:

- *approach* to service planning – how systematic the planning and review of service initiatives is
- *deployment* of service initiatives – whether the library service activities are systematically implemented throughout the entire organization.

When assessing service achievements, the library service will be identifying its:

- *results* – whether its performance is continually improving
- *scope* of the results – whether results cover all relevant areas of the organization.

Scoring the self-assessment facilitates benchmarking, in that the library and information service can easily identify those areas of the service that are performing poorly compared with other areas of the service and other library organizations. These results can then be used as a basis for establishing and operating a benchmarking programme, something which is discussed in Chapter 6, pages 142–4. However, scoring the self-assessment can present a danger in that some managers may latch onto the scores and not recognize the benefits of self-assessment as a planning tool. Some public sector organizations have tiered their models, thus removing the scoring process, but retaining the measure with which to assess continuous improvement. One demonstrator authority commented that while the scores were useful as an internal tool, they wished to avoid formalizing the scoring process because 'it would detract from the real benefits of the process'.

Stage three: Training

Any library and information service considering self-assessment should ensure that its staff receive adequate training to undertaken the task efficiently and effectively. Three levels of training programmes will be required:

- awareness-raising for those staff not formally involved in the process
- assessment-team training
- lead-officer training.

Van der Wiele et al (1995, 103) identified training as a key learning point of those organizations that had implemented self-assessment: 'the people who will undertake the self-assessment will have to be trained'.

The resource pack accompanying this book contains all the necessary documents to use in developing a training programme on self-assessment for library and information services. Section 2 of the pack outlines six training sessions, which provide a structured approach to introducing the concepts and techniques of self-assessment. The pack covers the whole self-assessment process from initial discussions on its potential value to the implementation of the toolkit and the post-assessment planning phase. Each outline provides guidance on key learning points, session content and overall objectives. Section 2 also provides copies of relevant overhead transparencies, session handouts and exercises. Table 5.4 summarizes the content of the various training workshops.

Table 5.4   *Content of self-assessment workshop sessions*

self-assessment

This session explores the concept of self-assessment in the context of the library and information sector. It provides step by step guidelines for planning library service self-assessment. The programme can be tailored for general awareness-raising or implemented as a wider assessment team training package.

Lead Officers / Senior Managers / Assessment Team / Library Staff

60 minutes

library and information sector improvement model

This session provides material for understanding the library and information sector improvement model. It can be used as a separate session for awareness raising with senior managers or for providing useful background and contextual information for the assessment team.

Lead Officers / Senior Managers / Assessment Team

75 minutes

the self-assessment criteria

This session explores the structure of the criteria and identifies the links within the assessment framework. It is intended for use with the assessment team as part of a comprehensive training programme.

Lead Officers / Assessment Team

75 minutes

the pro-forma approach to self-assessment

This session provides guidelines for undertaking a pro-forma approach to self-assessment. It is intended for use with the assessment team as part of a comprehensive training programme.

Lead Officers / Assessment Team

160 minutes

scoring the self-assessment

This session will introduce the scoring process for self-assessment. The session can be tailored for explaining the self-assessment score to senior managers or used as a whole package with the assessment team.

Lead Officers / Senior Managers / Assessment Team

105 minutes

action planning from self-assessment

This session examines the links between self-assessment and business planning. It provides guidelines for post-assessment planning. Again, it can be used for awareness raising with senior managers or with the assessment team.

Lead Officers / Senior Managers / Assessment Team

30 minutes

The training pack has been developed to ensure flexibility in approach and application. There are opportunities to tailor each session to suit the requirements of the individual library and information service. The pack can be used as a whole training course to be completed over two days, or as short course material to be used in one- or two-hour sessions. It is anticipated that the lead manager of the assessment will be responsible for the delivery of the training package.

Stage four: Planning the actual assessment

So far this chapter has concentrated on addressing those issues which need to be resolved before the assessment process can begin. This section looks at the mechanics of the assessment, that is, the roles attributed to team members, the breakdown of the assessment, and the timing of the process.

Before the self-assessment is carried out, it must be decided whether the library and information service is assessed as an entity, or whether separate units undertake individual assessments. Assessing each unit individually may provide a more in-depth analysis of the operational procedures within the library and information service. Unit assessment also offers a useful means of increasing employee involvement in the process (Zaremba and Crew, 1997). However, there is a danger in taking this approach in a first assessment, namely that the number of issues to address will far outreach the capabilities of the library service. Many of the mechanisms to support these improvements may not be in place, simply because a more general assessment was not undertaken. Once team members are used to the assessment process, it will then be possible to look at separate sections for benchmarking purposes.

Table 5.5 summarizes the various options available to the assessment team on how to approach the assessment. Each option has various time- and resource-related implications. Option one is useful for those teams that have difficulty in coordinating diaries, as after the initial training programme only one validation meeting is required. However, this approach is resource-intensive in that each team member will effectively be repeating the assessment undertaken by other members. Although there may be an advantage in this cross-validation, for a first assessment it is worth considering an alternative approach, simply because team members may prefer to have the support of the lead officer at hand. The issues raised in option one can also be considered appropriate for option two, although the scoring process is likely to employ staff time more effectively.

Table 5.5   *Options for undertaking self-assessment.*

option one	option two
• individual team members assess each criterion separately • individual members score assessment separately • meeting to validate results	• individual team members assess each criterion separately • assessment team scores results together

option three	option four
• assessment team go through each criterion together • lead officer scores assessment • meeting to validate results	• assessment team go through each criterion together • assessment team scores results together

Option three places more demands on staff time, although only one team member is drawn on to score the results. Option four takes a full-team approach to the assessment and scoring, and is perhaps the best route to take for the first assessment, since the lead officer will be able to guide the team through the process.

The timing of the assessment is critical. As a planning tool, it is suggested that the process begins four months before annual library and information plans must be agreed by committee or senior management. Figure 5.1 summarizes the timescale involved in assessment planning and implementation.

Stage five: Self-assessment

The key question which arose during the self-assessment was 'what constitutes evidence?'. Each approach to self-assessment expects the library and information service in question to identify relevant activities and initiatives, and to determine how far these reflect best practice. While it is possible to undertake a self-assessment based purely on 'gut feeling', the most effective approach is to identify what evidence the library and infor-

month one	• awareness-raising	• assessment planning *aims, objectives, model, method*
month two	• assessment-team training	• assessment planning *deployment, team roles*
month three	• self-assessment	• consensus meeting *areas for improvement* *action planning*
month four	• delivery of post-assessment plans	

Fig. 5.1   *Timescale involved in undertaking self-assessment*

mation service can use to prove that service planning and review is efficient and effective. This evidence may be in the form of plans, reports, newsletters, strategies, etc. Examples of relevant evidence are included in the criteria.

The actual process of self-assessment may alert the service to areas that need addressing. If, for example, the assessment team are aware of initiatives, but are unable to answer specific questions relating to them, then the communication of initiatives may need to be addressed.

The demonstrator authorities were also concerned with the question of how recently service initiatives or relevant activities had to be undertaken to warrant inclusion in the self-assessment. Again, these types of issues can be useful indicators of strengths and weaknesses in the current planning approach. If the assessment identifies that decisions are based on old and out-of-date information or one-off small-scale projects, then these will be areas where improvements need to be made.

Stage six: Scoring

The final stage of the self-assessment is the scoring of the evidence. The issues to consider when making the decision whether or not to score the process were discussed earlier in this chapter. This section addresses the practicalities of the scoring process and offers some suggestions on how to achieve a consensus score.

Scoring self-assessment is generally considered to be the most complex part of the actual assessment process. However, if the guidelines provided in the training pack and toolkit are followed, then the process is very straightforward. The assessment team must look at the evidence gathered during the actual process and decide the extent to which this reflects best practice. The evidence is scored on a scale of 0 to 100. A score of 0 means that the library and information service approach does not reflect best practice at all. A score of 100 means that all available evidence shows that the approach taken by the service is considered to be best practice in every respect.

The toolkit presents two tables that summarize the score. The first shows the breakdown of the planning score, and the second the breakdown of the scoring range for service achievements. If this is closely followed then the assessment team should have no difficulty in identifying an overall score for the library and information service.

ACHIEVING CONSENSUS

In the scoring process, there may be a varied range in the values of scores allocated to specific criteria. It is not uncommon when scoring in teams for a degree of diversity in scores to occur. This can usually be attributed to a number of factors:

- the position of the team member in the library and information service
- an inherent inconsistency in the deployment of service initiatives - if team members are drawn from across the organization, good and bad practice may be identified
- a diversity of understanding of good practice and/or the score card
- team members are unwilling to be critical or generous about service initiatives.

If the team members undertake the training session in the pack, then they should already have defined their parameters for the scoring process. In order to achieve a consensus score there are a number of steps the team should take, summarized in Figure 5.2.

step one	identify those scores that tally, and leave them
step two	identify those scores with small variations *between two points on the scale*
step three	using the score card as a basis for discussion, identify why there is a variation in score and agree consensus
step four	identify those scores with large variations *more than two points on the scale*
step five	re-visit the evidence and re-score
	identify why there is a variation in the score and agree consensus

Fig. 5.2   *Steps to achieve a consensus score*

Barriers to self-assessment

The experience of those public library and information sector organizations which have already implemented quality management and assessment programmes has highlighted a number of barriers to their successful implementation (Jones, Kinnell and Usherwood, 1998b).

EMPLOYEES

- unconvinced leaders who are unwilling to promote or support the process
- managers' inability to cope with new management techniques within the context of service restructuring and budget cuts
- defensive or cynical staff who are unwilling to change or try new ideas.

ATTITUDES

- unquestioning attitudes towards the validity of the initiative within the organization context: managers often fail to determine whether the goal is appropriate for their organization
- managers having a degree of complacency or self-satisfaction about what the organization has achieved and what it needs to achieve, ie they see no reason for change.

PLANNING

- a lack of clarity in what the organization hopes to achieve
- lack of time to embed quality into the culture of the library service.

APPROACH

- failing to imagine what it might be possible to achieve in the push for quality, or how quality should be defined in different sectors.

In addition, Holloway (1995, 406) adds:

- data collection being too superficial or too detailed
- those who don't like the results discrediting the framework or the process.

Responding to problems

From the list above it is possible to identify two key factors that can influence the smooth running of a self-assessment process: first, the inherent attitudes and beliefs of those who are charged with undertaking self-assessment; and second, the poor planning and lack of preparation prior to the self-assessment. This lack of preparation and planning will ultimately impact on how self-assessment is perceived and understood across the service. Library and information managers can ensure that they add value when implementing new initiatives such as self-assessment by ensuring that they fit in with what is already happening, and having mechanisms in place to measure the impact of the new approach.

There is also a need to acknowledge the fears of employees and address any concerns that might arise. One of their biggest concerns is likely to be how self-assessment will impact on their normal working practices and routine. It is important to stress that the process of self-assessment isn't about increasing workloads: it's about ensuring the efficiency and effectiveness of working practices.

One of the key benefits of the self-assessment process is that members of staff will 'own' the assessment. Staff will have identified the strengths, weaknesses and future priorities which must be acted on (Jones, Kinnell and Usherwood, 1999).

Critical success factors

From discussions with the demonstrator services and practitioners who have already undertaken self-assessment, it is possible to identify a number of critical success factors for the self-assessment process (Jones, Kinnell and Usherwood, 1998b; Jones, Kinnell and Usherwood, 1999).

Communication

Critical to the successful implementation of self-assessment is having appropriate communication strategies and systems in place. All stakeholders need to know how the initiative will help, what benefits it will bring, and their role in supporting the assessment. There are a number of issues which the library and information service must address:

- An effective communication strategy should involve everyone within the library service, and also key external stakeholders. However, careful consideration must be given to the issue of what information particular groups or individuals should be provided with. It is important that information is targeted to the right audience.
- Having a two-way communication strategy in place means that the library and information service must be willing to act on what is said. The organization can't pay lip-service to communication - it must be shown to act on the results of consultation.
- The lead managers of the process must endeavour to adopt an open and honest approach in the assessment (TQMI, 1995), not just in terms of the critique of library practices or through the process of sharing what is found with all relevant parties, but ensuring that all members of staff are aware of self-assessment and the possible benefits and impacts it might bring.

Human resource factors

The handling of human resource issues is another critical success factor in the self-assessment process. The concerns of all staff members should be addressed; however, it is the commitment of those members of staff who are directly involved in the assessment that is paramount:

- Senior managers must be visibly involved in the process, not only by providing the resources to undertake the assessment, but also by being willing to act on the results of the assessment.
- Staff need to be trained in the assessment process, they must understand the assessment approach in terms of its structure, content and professional context. If training is not provided then it is likely that the full benefits of the process will not be realized.
- The concerns of all staff members must be acknowledged and addressed, before, during and after the assessment process.

Managing the process

There are also a number of critical success factors inherent in the planning and preparation of the self-assessment:

- The implementation must be carefully planned. The library and information manager must ensure that there are appropriate strategies in place to ensure that the process runs smoothly.
- The approach taken in the self-assessment must suit the culture and experience of quality management within the organization.
- At each stage of the process, feedback from those involved should be obtained in order to deal with problems as and when they arise.
- There need to be mechanisms to ensure that the results of the process are fed back into the planning structure of the library and information service, and that these results are acted upon.
- Self-assessment should not be regarded as a static project. To gain real benefits the process must be repeated year on year to identify gains in efficiency and effectiveness. Quick benefits should be identified and worked towards while longer-term strategies are being put into place.

Summary and conclusions

In order for self-assessment to be successfully implemented, it was found by the demonstrator services that care had to be exercised in its implementation. Crucially, managers needed to have some training in applying the techniques. There also had to be an acceptance that investment in the process was essential for there to be real benefits over the longer term as well as in the short term. This was not just a once-for-all project but an ongoing process of monitoring, auditing and managing change for the benefit of the organization and its stakeholders. The mechanisms and techniques for ensuring that self-assessment is long-lived are considered in the next chapter.

References

Black, S A and Crumbley, H C (1997) Self-assessment: what's in it for us?, *Total Quality Management*, **8** (2/3), 90-3.

BQF (1997) *Guide to self-assessment: public sector guidelines*, British Quality Foundation.

Conti, T (1997) *Organisational self-assessment*, Chapman & Hall.

FEFC (1997) *Validating self-assessment*, Reference number 97/12, FEFC.

Hakes, C (1994) *Corporate self-assessment handbook*, Chapman & Hall.

Holloway, B (1995) Gaining the benefits of self-assessment, *Quality World*, (June), 404-6.

Jones, K, Kinnell, M and Usherwood, B (1998a) Self-assessment for quality management: a useful management tool or just management hype?, *Public Library Journal*, **13** (3), 33-7.

Jones, K, Kinnell, M, and Usherwood, B (1998b) *Assessment tools for quality management in public libraries: report of the first project workshop*, Department of Information and Library Studies, Loughborough University.

Jones, K, Kinnell, M and Usherwood, B (1999) *Planning for public library improvement: report of the second project workshop*, Department of Information and Library Studies, Loughborough University.

Jurow, S and Barnard, S B (1993) *Integrating total quality management in a library setting*, The Haworth Press, Inc.

Milner, E, Kinnell, M and Usherwood, B (1997) Quality management and public library services. In Brockman, J (ed) *Quality management and benchmarking in the information sector*, Bowker-Saur.

Pfeffer, N and Coote, A (1991) *Is quality good for you?*, Institute of Public Policy Research.

Reed, D (1995) Public test on the award model, *UK Quality*, (September), 10-11.

Reed, D (1997) *Public sector excellence research report*, British Quality Foundation.

Stewart, J and Walsh, K (1989) *The search for quality*, Local Government Training Board.

TQMI (1995) *What is self-assessment?: Your handbook*, TQM International.

TQMI (1997) *Managing a self-assessment process*, TQM International.

Van der Wiele, T et al. (1995) A study of progress in Europe's leading organisations in quality management practices, *International Journal of Quality and Reliability Management*, **13** (1), 84-104.

Van der Wiele, T et al. (1996) Quality management self-assessment: an examination in European business, *Journal of General Management*, **22** (1), 48-67.

Whitford, B and Bird, R (1996) *The pursuit of quality: how organisations in the UK are attaining excellence through quality certification and total quality management systems*, Prentice-Hall.

Wright, A (1997) Public service quality: lessons not learned, *Total Quality Management*, **8** (5), 313-20.

Zaremba, D and Crew, T (1997) Increasing involvement in self-assessment: the Royal Mail approach, *The TQM Magazine*, **7** (2), 29-32.

6
Self-assessment and the planning process

Introduction

The discussion in previous chapters has shown that a persistent problem in the implementation of new initiatives in the public information and library sector is ensuring their continuous use and upkeep. Unless the benefits of new management techniques can be quickly realized and identified, they often fall into abeyance. Correctly applied, however, self-assessment can foster the maintenance of quality initiatives within library and information services (Jones, Kinnell and Usherwood, 1998). An inherent principle is that self-assessment should act as a facilitator to service development. The action of undertaking the assessment invites the library and information manager to evaluate service strengths and weaknesses against explicit best-practice criteria. As a result, a great deal of scope is gained for the identification of improvement opportunities and areas for future consideration on the part of the library and information service. This chapter looks at the post-assessment actions that managers can undertake in order to ensure that self-assessment becomes the underlying framework for the way in which the service is reviewed, improved and developed.

Outcomes of the self-assessment process

Once the self-assessment proper is completed, the assessment team will have identified a number of critical issues relating to how the library service plans, implements, reviews and improves its activities. This is summarized in Table 6.1.

Table 6.1 *Outcomes of the self-assessment process*

For each **enabler** criterion the assessment team will have gathered evidence relating to:
- how effectively service activities are planned
  and deployed across the service   *and how this compares with best practice*
- the current strengths and weaknesses in
  their planning approaches

For each **results** criterion the assessment team will have gathered evidence relating to:
- the scope and spread of service performance data   *and how this compares with best practice*
- the current strengths and weaknesses inherent
  in their performance

To ensure that self-assessment is more than just an audit of how service activities compare with best practice, it is necessary for appropriate structures to be put into place to support and facilitate the creation of post-assessment improvement plans and actions. Unless this process is adequately planned, there is a real danger that the breadth and depth of issues to address may overwhelm the library and information manager. It is essential that the library service knows what its priorities are, as Black and Crumbley (1997, 91) argue:

> Faced with a list of hundreds of improvement issues, there is a temptation to do one of five things, do anything, do everything, do nothing, do the first things on the list first, do the easiest things first.

This can only lead to disjointed and uncoordinated improvement efforts which belie the best practice approach the library and information service is seeking to adopt. Self-assessment can provide the mechanisms with which to foster good planning practice across library and information services. At a basic level, self-assessment provides a review of service performance. The next stage of the planning cycle would be to ensure that this evidence is used to inform future plans, thereby leading to more effective working practices and procedures across the service.

Reviewing the self-assessment process

Before turning in more detail to the connection between self-assessment and service planning, it is worth looking at a number of practical issues which the assessment team and lead officer will need to address as a result of the assessment:

- the communication of the assessment outcomes
- the review of the assessment process.

Communication of results

Strategies should be in place to ensure that relevant stakeholders are informed about the outcomes of the assessment:

- Senior managers and resource providers should be informed of the key outcomes of the self-assessment process, ie where the general strengths and weaknesses lie. This type of consultation is also vital if resource requirements are highlighted by the assessment. Self-assessment provides useful evidence for these types of discussion, because it offers an objective assessment of where the service fits against current models of best practice.
- The library staff should also be informed of the results of the assessment. In some instances this can be used as a basis for training days or in-service discussions; for example, using the self-assessment criteria as a basis for discussions on the types of improvements required in employee management, and to identify potential solutions.
- Consideration should be given as to whether to discuss the results with the customers of the service. Here, it is not important to explain the mechanics of the assessment process, it is enough to identify the issues that the service is seeking to address and to open a wider dialogue.

- The library service should also consider whether to inform library suppliers or partners of the results of the assessment process, particularly in relation to the resource-management criterion where working relationships with partners and suppliers are addressed.

The focus of these discussions should not be on the 'score' the library and information service achieved in the assessment, but on those critical issues highlighted during the appraisal. The results of the assessment can be used as the basis of a wider dialogue with the key stakeholders. Again, self-assessment affords the opportunity to develop good practice within the organization, by developing a broader ownership of the results of the service and involving more internal and external stakeholders in the decision-making process. It also provides an ideal opportunity for the service to promote its commitment to meeting stakeholders' needs efficiently and effectively.

However, in the case of a first self-assessment, discussing results with external stakeholders might provide more areas for improvement than the service can realistically deal with. This is a critical issue: while it is important to discuss the development of the service with stakeholders, involving them in assessment and improvement discussions at an early stage might lead to unrealistic expectations. In order to ensure that the self-assessment is long-lived, it is best to identify realistic short-term goals and targets. By initially focusing on quick benefits, the library service is not only able to prove to stakeholders its increasing efficiency and effectiveness, but that the self-assessment process is a useful and valuable service-development tool.

If the library and information service is facing a compulsory self-assessment, then it is likely that the way in which results should be reported to senior managers will be dictated to the service. In some instances, eg in the case of Best Value, this may demand a scored assessment, with no additional information. The disadvantage of this approach is that there is little opportunity to discuss what the implications of these results are, and like much of the criticism directed at school performance league tables, it does little to emphasize the context within which the service is operating (Carvell, 1997). However, this library and information service will still have the actual data from self-assessment and will be able to use it to identify service development options.

Reviewing the self-assessment process

Another post-assessment action the assessment team should undertake is a review of the actual self-assessment process. Here, two critical issues will need to be addressed:

- how the mechanics of the assessment worked within the service
- how the assessment has impacted on the service.

Again, this post-assessment review helps set the standards of good management practice within the library and information service by ensuring that lessons are learned and acted upon. The assessment team should address:

- those issues requiring further clarification, eg criteria or the scoring process
- the bottlenecks in the process, eg training requirements, data collection, scoring
- the costs involved in undertaking the assessment, eg staff time, resources.

The focus should be on identifying those areas which cause difficulties for the assessment team and identifying possible solutions to ensure that the next self-assessment is undertaken more effectively (Hakes, 1994).

The second issue relating to the review of the self-assessment process, that of identifying its impact on the library and information service, is a crucial factor in deciding whether or not to continue with self-assessment. Critically, two aspects should be considered:

- the reaction of staff to the assessment process
- the impact of the assessment on the effectiveness of the service.

When taking account of employee attitudes to self-assessment, it is vital that lessons are learned and that the process is taken forward and improved. Part of this procedure will involve dealing with the cynicism of those staff who 'have seen it all before' and don't believe that the system will change. If staff are overtly negative, the reasons for these attitudes must be identified and acted upon. Table 6.2 highlights a number of reasons why staff might be sceptical of the process after the assessment has taken place.

Table 6.2 *Reasons for post-assessment scepticism*

Reasons for scepticism	Possible solutions
findings won't be acted upon	• identify quick benefits • ensure that any resulting changes are linked to the self-assessment
findings will be acted upon	• ensure that staff understand that self-assessment is about continuous improvement – not about identifying faults • ensure that improvements are implemented gradually with appropriate training courses and communication strategies attached
language used in assessment	• use as opportunity to train staff in management practices across the public sector • identify real difficulties and adapt the language

The second aspect to consider is the impact of the self-assessment on the efficiency and effectiveness of the service. The basic tenet of self-assessment is that it should act as a service development tool. If, therefore, improvement activities are implemented, it should be possible to determine how far these activities have increased the efficiency of the service. A basic way to judge whether this has occurred or not is through an improved score in the second self-assessment. Whether the service does in fact improve against the LISIM, however, depends on how the results of the assessment are used to inform the planning process.

Linking self-assessment and planning

Strategic and service-level planning is becoming an increasingly vital role of library and information managers. A prime example is the recent requirement for all public library authorities to provide annual library plans to the DCMS. However, within other public information organizations there are now growing pressures from outside agencies to implement effective planning structures; for example, Next Step agencies work within strict performance-assessment criteria laid down by government ministers (Walsh, 1995).

One of the strengths of the LISIM is that it provides a framework for business planning. It identifies the types of activities that should be considered when identifying potential service enhancements. The LISIM does not offer a mechanistic planning structure for the public information and library sector, it offers a flexible framework for those services seeking to increase the efficiency and effectiveness of the way in which their services are provided to disparate groups of stakeholders. Conti (1997, 173-4) suggests that when the process is fully aligned with the normal planning cycle in the service, self-assessment affords the opportunity to:

- perform critical analyses of progress
- identify the causes of deviations from original plans
- introduce any variations in goals
- verify the state of capabilities in relation to the new set of goals.

Figure 6.1 shows the various stages in the post-assessment planning process. These individual stages are then discussed in more detail.

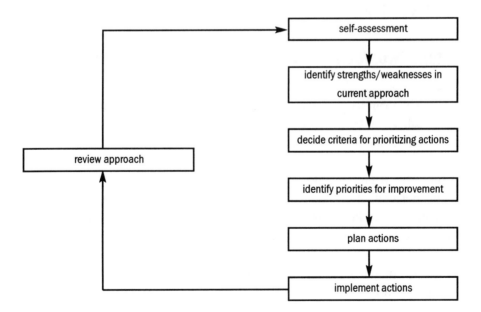

Fig. 6.1   *Action planning from self-assessment, derived from BQF (1997, 73)*

Stage one: List strengths and weaknesses

The identification of service strengths and weaknesses is an inherent part of the self-assessment process. There are two key areas where improvement issues will arise:

- issues which need to be addressed as a result of the assessment, eg the need to review internal communications
- issues which need to be addressed as a result of the scoring process, eg an overall weakness in the deployment of service activities.

Given that it is not unusual to identify numerous issues to address in a self-assessment, it is worth sorting them into related categories in order to begin the process of prioritizing actions. For example, one could identify all development issues regarding:

- internal communication
- the poor spread or deployment of initiatives
- the management of employees
- customer-facing services
- key processes.

Stage two: Identify criteria for prioritizing actions

> The main issue with an improvement plan is to define priorities against a balance of business strategy, current activities, resource constraints and an understanding of the model. (Wright, 1997, 91)

Once the parameters for prioritizing performance improvements have been defined, the action planning process is very straightforward. The Britsh Quality Foundation (1997, 73) has identified a number of factors to take into account when considering service options:

- The current service plans, priorities and strategies in place; for example, a library service implementing a new computer system might decide to address issues identified in the resource management sub-criteria relating to the management of information technology.

- The priorities of the parent organization can also influence what actions the library and information service decides to take - local authority, health service trust or government department. For example, if a university is seeking to improve student access to information technology in order to support the educational process, the university library might seek to improve the management of its IT resources.
- The resources available for service developments. This is a critical factor: improvement actions cannot be undertaken unless there are resources available to implement them. In some instances, where problem areas are identified because of obvious funding shortfalls, then the results might be used to lobby senior managers on the need for extra resources.
- If the self-assessment highlights a critical failing in a key process, then that should become a key priority for change.
- Stakeholder priorities for improvement can also be used to inform discussions.
- Match against assessment criterion. However, what is an important criterion to one organization may be less so to another.

While self-assessment results can have a role to play in informing improvement decisions, there is a danger that the service will fall into the trap of focusing on improving scores rather than on improving working practices and procedures. However, scores can indicate general issues relating to the way in which services are planned. For example, a low score might indicate that there are significant gaps in the feedback of service reviews into planning cycles. A higher score might suggest that the service should focus more on improvement planning and ensuring that stakeholder satisfaction is addressed across the whole organization.

Stage three: Identify priorities for improvement

Once the parameters for choosing service priorities have been identified, it is then necessary to determine which issues to tackle. While the criteria for prioritizing were discussed above, it is also necessary to:

- distinguish between long- and short-term objectives
- align the improvement activities to current implementation plans.

It is suggested that a cross section of staff take part in the improvement discussions, as implementing their own ideas is likely to facilitate more effective improvements (Karlsson and Wiklund, 1997).

Ensuring continuous improvement against the LISIM is a long-term commitment on the part of the library and information service. Not only will the progression involve a cultural change across the organization, but it will necessitate a great deal of time and effort to ensure that the improvements are sustained. As a result, it is necessary to identify and distinguish between long- and short-term objectives for improvement plans. In some instances, where there has been no previous activity - for example, the demonstrator services' lack of evidence relating to employee satisfaction - then actions necessary to address these issues may seem daunting. Consequently it is necessary to identify quick benefits, actions that will reap rewards in the short term, while longer-term strategies are put in place. It is better to try to start improvement strategies somewhere, even if it seems insignificant; for example, monitoring staff turnover can provide a simple but effective measure of employee satisfaction. Sutton, quoted in Weingand (1997, 64) suggests that 'short-term problem-solving in the context of long range planning is a powerful motivator at every level of the organisation'. Table 6.3 provides examples of long- and short-term activities in relation to improving the way in which the achievements of the library service are measured.

It is also necessary to identify those actions which will have a significant impact on the culture of the library and information service: in particular, those long-term strategic actions which will have implications for service delivery. By implementing improvements, the library and information manager must recognize that the expectations and demands of stakeholders will undoubtedly increase.

Knowing where improvement plans align to current plans is also essential. It may avoid duplication of effort, and in those instances where improvements are not a priority it will avoid unnecessary activity on the part of the service.

Table 6.3 *Long- and short-term improvement targets*

	Quick benefits	Medium-term targets	Long-term targets
Customer satisfaction	Using available management information to predict satisfaction, eg % of requests met, return visits.	Establishing internal mechanisms to solicit feedback from users, eg comments cards.	Implementing strategies for identifying customer perceptions, eg annual surveys, customer forums.
Employee satisfaction	Using available management information to predict satisfaction, eg absenteeism, staff turnover.	Establishing internal mechanisms to solicit feedback from employees, eg appraisal, exit interviews	Implementing strategies for identifying employee perceptions of job satisfaction, eg annual surveys, employee forums.
Impact on society	Using available management information to predict impact on society, eg post-code analysis of membership.	Establishing internal mechanisms to identify impact on society, eg performance indicators / targets, media watching.	Implementing strategies for identifying impact on society, eg forums, focus groups.
Overall performance	Using available management information to predict performance, eg response rates.	Establishing internal mechanisms to identify overall performance, eg performance indicators.	Implementing strategies for identifying overall performance, eg forums, focus groups.

Once these decisions have been taken, it will be possible to list the strengths and weaknesses of the service according to the criteria identified by Hakes (1994):

- activities to *maintain* at their current attainment level
- activities to *exploit* in order to develop them further
- activities to *acknowledge* as problematic
- activities to *improve*.

It isn't uncommon to identify hundreds of areas for improvement in a self-assessment, and therefore it is vital that consensus is gained on the right issues to address. These decisions can be made as part of planning process, if the self-assessment is timed correctly. In the public library sector for example, the DCMS planning guidelines expect a SWOT analysis to be undertaken, and that the self-assessment will provide sufficient evidence to identify the strengths and weaknesses of the service (DCMS, 1997).

Stage four: Plan actions

Once it has been decided what actions are necessary to ensure the development of the library and information service, then it is necessary to plan the actions required to implement the changes. Again, these actions are merely good practice. For each activity the library and information manager must endeavour to ensure that:

- key tasks are defined and understood
- necessary actions are listed
- accountabilities for each action are defined and accepted
- performance targets for each action are set
- performance measures for each action are identified and documented
- mechanisms are in place to review the achievement of targets and to feed the review into future planning activities
- timescales for each activity are set.

Stage five: Implement actions

Again, ensure that strategies are in place to inform staff about any changes that are taking place. Communication is a critical success factor of the quality-improvement process, and is essential if the ongoing support of the staff is to be gained (Porter and Parker, 1993).

Stage six: Review

The final stage of the post-assessment planning process is the review of what has been achieved, in terms of:

- whether the objectives have been reached
- whether the performance targets have been met

- whether the planned timescales have been achieved.

The manager will also be looking for evidence of improved results in the next self-assessment. It is important to recognize that continuous improvement is just that, it is a 'perpetually moving target' (Weingand, 1997, 106). Self-assessment can only really benefit organizations if it is undertaken year-on-year rather than as a one-off initiative. As Dalrymple and Donnelly (1997, 132) suggest when discussing self-assessment in the public sector, 'the needs of customers and other stakeholders change, sometimes rapidly, over time and periodic audits against the model may help to track these changes and enable timely service redesign and development.'

Table 6.4 summarizes the various post-assessment plans and strategies the demonstrator services adopted.

Table 6.4   *Demonstrator authority post-assessment action plans*

	Library service A	Library service B
communication	• elected members • head of library service • library management team • marketing manager • managers of key processes – develop ownership	• senior management team • managers of key processes
review	• process • criteria • method	• process • criteria • method
post-assessment actions	• planning review seminars	• action plan for improvement against each criterion

Tools for post-assessment planning

A common problem for organizations wishing to act on the results of their self-assessment is that they are unsure of how to start the improvement process. The previous section discussed the action-planning process; this section offers some techniques for determining which actions are critical and which are of secondary importance. Five common techniques that can be used when implementing quality improvements in library and information services are defined and summarized.

Benchmarking (process-improvement tool)

DEFINITION

Benchmarking is the comparison and review of service performance or processes against best-in-class organizations. The aim is to identify and implement possible areas for improvement. Benchmarking is an inherent concept of the self-assessment process. A significant proportion of a scored assessment is determined by comparison against best-in-class services. There are two key types of benchmarking: the comparison of results, and the comparison of processes. For the learning organization it is the comparison of processes which should offer the most reward, as Andersen and Pettersen (1996, 6) suggest:

> If learning, motivating and improvement are to be the result of a benchmarking study, it requires that the causes for the performance gaps are the focus of attention. The process itself has to be analysed.

Within the library and information sector, benchmarking affords the 'opportunity for new thinking about what are realistic and feasible targets' (Jurow, 1993, 12).

RESOURCE REQUIREMENTS

- coordinator/manager
- staff
- time
- consumables.

PROCESS

- The first stage in the benchmarking process is to identify what aspects of the organization need to be benchmarked. Self-assessment will help identify two key aspects: issues relating to performance, such as low levels of customer satisfaction, and issues relating to key functions, such as the poor deployment of key processes.

- Once each area for improvement has been identified, it is then necessary to document the process; the flow-chart method later in this section, provides useful guidelines for this.
- The manager should then seek to identify appropriate best practice to benchmark against. This might be internal or external. In some instances the self-assessment will flag up where pockets of good practice exist within the library and information service. Benchmarking is an ideal opportunity to ensure that lessons are learned and shared across the whole service.
- External benchmarking need not necessarily be against best-in-class, ie another library and information service; when benchmarking specific functions, such as book delivery, it might be worth identifying those organizations which implement similar functions, such as parcel delivery services.
- The next phase involves learning from the benchmarking partner about how they implement their processes. This involves actually understanding what the organization does, and why it carries out specific activities (Andersen and Pettersen, 1996, 17). Various methods can be used to learn about processes, eg questionnaires, interviews, visits. The key success factor is that sufficient evidence relating to the management of the process is identified.
- Once the best-practice organization's processes are understood, the library and information service can then seek to identify the gaps between best practice and its own activities. Once the gaps have been identified it is then necessary to assess why these gaps have occurred.
- The lessons learned from the best-practice organization can then be implemented into the processes of the library and information service.
- A critical success factor of self-assessment is that benchmarking is a continuous year-on-year process.

STAFF INVOLVEMENT

Communication of benchmarking activities is a key issue. Where processes are benchmarked it is vital that those responsible for managing the process within the library and information service are involved in the benchmarking programme.

Value

Benchmarking can support service development and improvement, and it can also be undertaken as a fulfilment of requirements in the self-assessment process.

Brainstorming (problem-solving technique)

Definition

The aim of brainstorming is to allow the free flow of ideas and suggestions between teams or groups who are concerned with solving specific problems.

Resource requirements

- facilitator
- staff : usually 8 – 12 staff in one session
- time: 15 minutes for brainstorming, 30 minutes discussion
- consumables.

Process

First phase

- Begin with a blank space – either a flip chart or board – in clear view of all participants.
- Define the subject to be brainstormed: 'the problem must be clearly stated and understood by all'. (Marsh, 1993, 17)
- Either allow for a few minutes' individual brainstorming or ask for contributions cold.
- Go round the room and ask for individual contributions. Participants should be free to offer contributions without reproach or ridicule. There should be no comments from other participants while this is taking place.

- When everyone has made their contribution, or the initial 15 minutes has passed, move on to the next part of the session – the discussion and analysis of problems.

SECOND PHASE

- During the post-brainstorm discussion it is vital for the facilitator to keep control of the group. Again, reproach or blame should be avoided. The aim of the session is to identify possible solutions to problems, and while this will involve the identification of their causes, their justification should be avoided.
- Edge (1990); Marsh (1993) suggest that for ease of analysis the problems should be classified into the following categories:
  - Those issues which the brainstorming team have total control over – for example, day-to-day procedures
  - Those issues where the brainstorming team has only partial control – for example, library plans and policies
  - Those issues where the brainstorming team has no control – for example, funding requirements.
- Within the timescale available it is advisable that the team first deal with those issues they are fully able to influence, then those issues where they have partial control, then move on to those issues where they will have no influence, but may have some suggestions for improvement.

STAFF INVOLVEMENT

A cross-section of staff can be easily involved in a brainstorming session. Indeed, the mix of front-line staff, supervisors and managers might provide a more effective and rounded discussion.

VALUE

Brainstorming enables more ideas and solutions to be identified than would be the case individually (Edge, 1990).

Flowcharting (process-mapping technique)

DEFINITION

Workflow diagrams are a process-mapping technique. The diagrams document the sequence of key activities and decisions which are undertaken when carrying out specific tasks. They can be used to identify bottlenecks in working practices and procedures.

RESOURCE REQUIREMENTS

- coordinator
- staff
- time
- training.

PROCESS

Using evidence from the self-assessment, identify key problem areas or working practices to be documented:

- Identify and list in sequence the various steps involved in undertaking the task. For each step, identify the key actions that take place – for example, whether decisions are taken – the inputs to the process and the outputs of the process.
- Document the links between each activity, process or output.
- Once the flowchart for the process is agreed, produce a final version.
- Identify clear problem areas and implement improvements.

STAFF INVOLVEMENT

Again, it is important that those members of staff involved in undertaking the activity are involved in creating the flow diagram.

VALUE

Flowcharts provide an overview of key working procedures and can quickly identify those stages in the sequence where there are issues to address.

Fishbone analysis (problem-solving technique)

DEFINITION

Fishbone analysis is a very useful problem-solving tool. It provides a succinct clarification of the key causes of a specific problem; indeed, fishbone analysis is also known as cause and effect analysis. It offers a useful technique for solving problems identified in Pareto analysis (see next section), or for identifying key issues for Pareto analysis. Fishbone analysis and brainstorming techniques often complement each other.

RESOURCE REQUIREMENTS

- facilitator
- staff
- training
- time: it can take more than one session to identify all causes and possible solutions
- consumables

PROCESS

- Identify the subject for analysis. As suggested above, this technique offers a useful follow-on for solving the critical problems identified through Pareto analysis.
- Draw a fishbone structure on a flip chart or board.

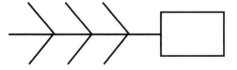

- In the 'head' of the fish define the problem or 'effect'.

- On each 'bone' identify key 'causes'. So, for example if the 'effect' is missing stock, problems might include mis-shelving, theft, wrong catalogue details.
- During this brainstorming process, key themes or generic issues should begin to emerge. It should be possible to label each 'bone'. Marsh (1993, 100) suggests that human resources, physical resources, inputs, internal factors, and external factors are likely to emerge as clear 'bones'.
- Conclude the brainstorm when all suggestions have been identified.
- Judge the degree to which each 'bone' causes the 'effect'. Those 'bones' with a high number of issues identified would suggest that there are inherent problems in this area that need to be addressed.
- Identify possible solutions and implement improvement actions.

STAFF INVOLVEMENT

As with brainstorming, a cross-section of staff will provide a useful overview of all issues that need to be considered. However it is important that senior managers are involved to ensure that any critical actions that are identified are moved forward.

VALUE

Fishbone analysis clarifies the possible causes of a particular problem.

Pareto analysis (process-improvement technique)

DEFINITION

The simple principle of Pareto analysis is that in most processes there are a few critical factors which will have a significant effect on their outcome and many insignificant factors which will have little bearing on the result. It is generally considered that 20% of effort causes 80% of effect. Pareto analysis enables organizations to identify those critical activities which have most impact, thereby offering a tool for the efficient and effective use of resources.

RESOURCE REQUIREMENTS

- data collection
- facilitator
- staff
- time
- training
- consumables.

PROCESS

- Identify a critical process that appears to be failing, such as the document delivery system.
- Collect relevant data relating to that process, using for example a list of complaints relating to specific categories.
- Map relevant data on a Pareto chart - mapping the causes on the x axis, with the percentage occurrence on the y axis.
- From the chart the principal cause of the problems will become apparent.
- This evidence can then be used to investigate the real, critical issue further; for example, a high level of complaints about stock availability might lead to a fishbone analysis of possible causes, eg lack of resources, mis-shelving etc.
- Identify possible solutions and implement improvement activities.

STAFF INVOLVEMENT

In Pareto analysis fewer staff will be involved in the initial stage. It is vital that those staff who take part are trained in basic statistical techniques.

VALUE

Pareto analysis can help to focus often scarce resources on critical improvement issues.

Maintaining self-assessment and continuous improvement

Maintaining the impetus in service development and improvement is perhaps the most crucial aspect of the post-assessment process. This means getting into the routine of continuous review and improvement, ensuring that lessons are learned and changes maintained. Part of this strategy will involve the implementation of improvement plans, which was discussed in the previous section. However, there are a number of additional factors that can impact on the successful maintenance of quality management initiatives (Jones, Kinnell and Usherwood, 1998), and these are discussed below.

While it is possible for the library and information service to undertake only one self-assessment, its founding principle is that the organization should learn from the evaluation and seek to improve its activities. In effect, self-assessment should become aligned to the annual planning cycle in the organization, identifying those strengths and weaknesses which the library and information service must seek to address.

Choosing the right approach

Developing inflexible models, and implementing initiatives which do not take account of the organizational context, plays a major part in the failure of quality programmes (Jones, Kinnell and Usherwood, 1998). It is essential that the library and information service understands what it wants to achieve and why it is adopting a particular route. It may be necessary to tailor the approaches to suit the organization's requirements, but care should be taken to ensure that the rigour of the approach is not lost. In some instances the organization may not know the right approach to service improvement unless it has tried and tested various alternatives. Therefore, piloting of different approaches is essential.

The first self-assessment will undoubtedly seem a daunting task, and it will be all too easy to give up, especially if numerous areas to address are identified. The biggest mistake an organization can make is not to act on the results identified in the self-assessment, and either abandon it altogether or leave it for another year to see if things have got any better.

However, if steps are taken to ensure that even low-level improvement planning takes place then the service will be able to reap the rewards.

The service context – the external environment

Another factor which will influence the maintenance of quality initiatives is the demands placed on the service through its external environment. Particularly when dealing with the often conflicting demands of various stakeholders, it is important to be aware of the context within which the service is operating. Within many organizations, the demand to constantly implement new initiatives can necessitate a great deal of time and effort, which might result in older initiatives falling into abeyance. In some instances it is the lack of immediate impact that leads to the abandonment of initiatives. The manager must ensure that all external stakeholders are informed of the process and its overarching aim, in order to ensure their support for what can be a long-term strategy. Knowing how self-assessment has impacted or might impact on service development is a critical tool in this process (Jones, Kinnell and Usherwood, 1999).

The service context – the internal environment

The internal environment of the library and information service will also impact on the maintenance of self-assessment. Self-assessment can have implications for resources, both physical and human. Staff time undertaking self-assessment cannot be used elsewhere. However, the impact on planning and development strategies would suggest that self-assessment doesn't add to work, it merely changes the way things are carried out. There are, however, direct financial costs which need to be considered as well.

Staff involvement

Staff involvement is fundamental to maintaining the impetus in quality initiatives. This process begins with the development of the initiatives by involving staff at all stages, and having mechanisms in place to achieve ownership. Such mechanisms include staff training and appraisal. Effective communication strategies are also required, so that problems can be dealt with quickly and efficiently. A key issue to be addressed is ensuring that self-assessment doesn't become too staid or monotonous. Again, making sure that improvements have been implemented should result in changes in the process and the outcome.

Identifying links to other strategies

During the development of the self-assessment toolkit, the demonstrator services were keen to identify how the LISIM compared with the other approaches to quality which were in use in the public sector: principally Investors in People and Charter Mark, because these were the models the services had either adopted or were investigating. At the same time, the DCMS produced its planning guidelines for public library authorities, and it was therefore also felt necessary to identify the possible fit between these and the LISM.

Knowing where there are links and overlaps between approaches provides a useful planning tool. Self-assessment can provide the necessary evidence for applying for external awards such as Investors in People and Charter Mark. It might also provide the necessary evidence with which to persuade senior managers of the value of such a process.

For those library and information services operating within an accreditation system, Table 6.5 also provides details of where overlaps between the LISIM and two major accreditation schemes for public information services occur.

Critical success factors for maintaining self-assessment

The following critical success factors for maintaining self-assessment in library and information services have been identified (Jones, Kinnell and Usherwood, 1998):

- Regarding self-assessment not as a static or one-off project, but acknowledging the need for acting on the outcomes with improvement plans and cycles.
- Aligning self-assessment with the planning structure of the library and information service; making it an integral part of the data-gathering process.

Table 6.5   *Links between the LISIM and other approches to quality, derived from BQF (1998)*

	quality awards		statutory requirement		accreditation process	
	Investors in People	Charter Mark	Business Excellence Model	DCMS Planning Guidelines	LINC	CoLRIC
Leadership	✓✓	✓	✓✓✓	✓	✓	✓✓
Policy and strategy	✓✓	✓✓	✓✓✓	✓✓✓	✓✓	✓✓
Customer focus	✓	✓✓✓	✓	✓✓	✓✓	✓✓
Employee management	✓✓✓	✓✓	✓✓✓	✓	✓✓	✓✓
Resource management	✓	✓✓	✓✓✓	✓✓	✓✓✓	✓✓✓
Processes	✓	✓	✓✓✓	✓	✓✓	✓
Customer satisfaction	✓	✓✓✓	✓✓✓	✓	✓	✓
Employee satisfaction	✓✓✓	✓✓	✓✓✓	✓	✓	✓
Impact on society	✓	✓✓	✓	✓	✓	✓
Overall performance	✓	✓	✓✓✓	✓✓	✓	✓

Key:
✓✓✓	strong overlap in approach, concepts and issues to address
✓✓	some overlap in approach, concepts and issues to address
✓	slight overlap in approach, concepts and issues to address
✓	no overlap in concepts and issues to address

- Having marketing strategies in place to create an awareness of what the library can do, thereby ensuring the support of key stakeholders for the process.

Summary and conclusions

This chapter has shown that self-assessment can support the planning process of library and information services. It enables managers to identify strengths and weaknesses in the way in which processes are managed and to plan corrective actions. A number of tools and techniques have been summarized to help facilitate this process. Post-assessment planning is the most critical aspect of the self-assessment process: it must be undertaken if the full benefits of this management technique are to be realized.

References

Andersen, B and Pettersen, P-G (1996) *The benchmarking handbook: step by step instructions*, Chapman & Hall.

Black, S A and Crumbley, H C (1997) Self-assessment: what's in it for us?, *Total Quality Management*, **8** (2/3),90-3.

BQF (1997) *Guide to self-assessment: public sector guidelines*, British Quality Foundation.

BQF (1998) *Quality links*, British Quality Foundation.

Carvell, J (1997) School results: shaming and acclaiming, *The Guardian G2*, (18 November), 2.

Conti, T (1997) *Organisational self-assessment*, Chapman & Hall.

Dalrymple, J F and Donnelly M (1997) Managing and evaluating customer complaint procedures in local government, *Total Quality Management*, **8** (2/3), 130-4.

DCMS (1997) *Annual library plan: guidelines*, Department of Culture Media and Sport.

Edge, J (1990) Quality improvement activities and techniques. In Lock, D (ed) *Gower handbook of quality management*, Gower.

Hakes, C (1994) *Corporate self-assessment handbook*, Chapman & Hall.

Jones, K, Kinnell, M and Usherwood, B (1998) *Assessment Tools for Quality Management in Public Libraries: report of the First Project Workshop*, Department of Information and Library Studies, Loughborough University.

Jones, K, Kinnell, M and Usherwood, B (1999) *Planning for public library improvement: report of the second project workshop*, Department of Information and Library Studies, Loughborough University.

Jurow, S (1993) Tools for measuring and improving performance. In Jurow, S and Barnard, S B (eds) *Integrating total quality management in a library setting*, The Haworth Press.

Karlsson, S and Wiklund, P S (1997) Critical aspects of quality method implementation, *Total Quality Management*, **8** (1), 55-65.

Marsh, J (1993) *The quality tool-kit: an A-Z of tools and techniques*, IFS International.

Porter, L J and Parker, A J (1993) Total quality management – the critical success factors, *Total Quality Management*, **4** (1), 13-22.

Walsh, K (1995) Quality through markets: the new public service management. In Wilkinson, A and Wilmott, H (eds) *Making quality critical: new perspectives on organizational change*, International Thomson Business Press.

Weingand, D E (1997) *Customer service excellence: a concise guide for librarians*, American Library Association.

Wright, A (1997) Public service quality: lessons not learned, *Total Quality Management*, **8** (5), 313-20.

7

Self-assessment in library and information services

It has prompted much debate and given us significant indicators of what and how to tackle the future. I would fully intend this to be an annual project to assess the development (of the service) and to use it as a base for our move to IiP.

(Chief Librarian, demonstrator authority)

Introduction

Previous work in the field has indicated that the poor take-up of total quality systems by library and information services has been related to perceptions of low relevance, 'faddism' and scepticism about the use of private sector management jargon and models (Milner, Kinnell and Usherwood, 1997). The toolkit presented in this book and the accompanying resource pack were developed using action-research techniques which enabled library practitioners to own and develop the process of adapting and tailoring quality management techniques to their specific organizational context. By using this methodology, a relevant tool has been developed, which acknowledges the need for stringent assessment, while at the same time placing this assessment within a broader understanding of the purpose of public sector organizations.

While this and other research (Reed, 1997; Samuels, 1998) has shown that many of the concepts of the mainstream self-assessment approaches, such as the Business Excellence Model, have relevance for the public sector, it is clear that practitioners still require and demand models and techniques specifically focused on their organization's needs. In some library and information sector organizations corporate demands might require use of the Business Excellence Model as opposed to the more tailored approaches of the LISIM. In such circumstances there is still a need to think carefully about the language and terminology used in the self-assessment. The LISIM can be of help through its profession-specific examples and terminology.

Through the action-research focus, it has also been possible to construct a model that meets the needs of library and information services, while also retaining the integrity of an approach which will support benchmarking across other public sector organizations. By combining a tailored yet generic approach to continuous improvement, the LISIM will provide practitioners with the tools necessary to meet the future challenges of managing in a changing public sector.

The techniques used to develop the model have ensured that the research influences, shapes and supports professional practice. As Winter (1996, 13) suggests, 'action research is seen as a way of investigating professional expertise which links practice and the analysis of practice into a single continuously developing sequence'. This chapter offers some final thoughts and recommendations for library and information professionals considering self-assessment.

Developing sector-specific self-assessment tools

The development of the LISIM is very timely for the public library and information sector. Given the increasing demands on public services to prove the efficient and effective use of resources through the use of management techniques such as self-assessment, a sector-specific model has the advantage of enabling library and information services to lead, rather than be pushed along by, the quality agenda. It also provides a useful planning framework, another area where library and information managers are under pressure to adopt more exacting and rigorous tools.

Library services can often bear the brunt of cut-backs within public sector organizations. The LISIM provides the framework for identifying evidence on the impact, relevance and value of the library and information service within the context of its management structure, whether it is local authority, government department, health care trust, university or college of further education.

Previous work within the library and information sector has demonstrated that there is a real need to tailor, adapt and customize those quality management tools and techniques that were originally developed in the private sector (Milner, Kinnell and Usherwood, 1997); not just to tack on public sector differences, but to accommodate the specific context of the public information and library sector. This kind of analysis must be pragmatic. It must match the benefits of private sector management approaches with the inherent values of library and information services. Lessons are to be learned and shared between the sectors. It is not a question of 'one-way traffic' from the private sector to the public sector as suggested by the populist 1980s management literature.

However, while there is a need to ensure that organizational contexts are accounted for in models of good management practice, care should be taken to ensure that these approaches are not tailored to the extent that the rigour of the approach is lost. For example, employee satisfaction results were not collected on a regular basis by any of the demonstrator services, yet the concept is inherent in the LISIM. Part of the move to self-assessment will involve a change in management culture and attitudes, and the appropriate use of management terminology and actions can help foster this approach.

Implementing self-assessment

The key lesson to draw from the experience of those organizations that have implemented quality tools and techniques is that unless the approach becomes part and parcel of how the library and information service manages its processes, there is every chance it will fall into abeyance. Quality management and self-assessment are not add-on initiatives, and those library services where they are perceived as such are in danger of losing the potential benefits they can provide. Efficient and effective management practices should be the basis of public library and information service provision: that is, the management and delivery of services should be continuously improved in order to sustain and develop the library and information service. These notions are also inherent principles of the self-assessment model identified in this book.

From the testimony of those managers in public sector organizations which have undertaken self-assessment there is no doubt that it can have a huge impact by improving and supporting the way in which services are managed and developed (Whitford and Bird, 1996). However, it is by no means a 'pain-free' process, and can require radical shifts in the attitudes, expectations and actions of those implementing self-assessment. Assessors must be prepared to critique how long-standing practices are carried out. They must also be prepared to act on these evaluations. Managers from both demonstrator services were convinced that the assessment had given them the opportunity to address such critical issues in a structured and coherent way. However, if this is to happen, as the discussions in Chapters 5 and 6 showed, the following internal and external factors must be acknowledged and addressed by the lead officer and the assessment team:

- The communication of the process must be geared to the needs of those learning about self-assessment, perhaps for the first time.
- For staff, the notion of self-assessment is likely to produce an element of fear and apprehension about the reason why self-assessment is being undertaken, and how the outcome will impact on them. It is important to emphasize that, while self-assessment is about identifying opportunities for improving the service, it is not about identifying scapegoats or appointing blame.
- Training in the self-assessment approach is vital if the process is to be completed comprehensively and efficiently.
- Senior managers must also be informed of the potential and value of self-assessment, not least because they are the ones who must support the post-assessment improvement activities.

A critical success factor of the self-assessment process is to ensure that it is planned and implemented correctly. Chapter 5 provides a detailed analysis of the issues which should be considered when planning the assessment. Unless the library and information service is sure about what it is trying to achieve, and how this will be accomplished, then there is a danger that the full potential of the tool will not be realized. Care must also be taken to ensure that self-assessment is appropriate to the specific circumstances within which the library service is operating: otherwise the process might be perceived as an added burden. One demonstrator library service put their self-assessment on hold because they did not have sufficient support for the process. The service was operating without a full senior management team and was facing restructuring due to budget cuts. Senior managers therefore felt that it would be inopportune to undertake the self-assessment. However, they also considered that self-assessment would be a useful tool to help the library and information service move forward, once these changes had been introduced.

Acting on self-assessment

> What is important is not the self-assessment exercise itself, but what you do following it. A self-assessment programme will not result in improvement on its own: what is required is action following up on the findings. (Wright, 1997, 320)

Self-assessment is not just an audit of where the library and information service fits against a model of good practice. The process also encourages practitioners to determine future improvement activities. It offers a catalyst to move the service forward. It supports the planning process by providing appropriate evidence of key problem areas as well as service achievements.

In order for self-assessment to be successfully integrated into planning processes, it was found that care had to be exercised in its implementation. Short-term strategies were put in place by the demonstrator services, in order to begin the process of developing and implementing longer-term changes. It was also recognized by the demonstrator services that investment in the process was essential for there to be real benefit over the longer term as well as in the short term. This was not just a once-and-for-all project but an ongoing process of monitoring, auditing and managing change for the benefit of the organization and its stakeholders.

Recommendations

This book and training pack provides an excellent example of the way in which research in the library and information sector can be used to inform professional practice. It offers clear guidelines for those library and information managers considering self-assessment. The following section offers some recommendations for the continuing use and development of self-assessment tools in the library and information sector.

1   The LISIM should be taken forward and adapted by the public library and information sector. Library and information practitioners should use the professional literature, electronic discussion lists and professional meetings such as the Public Library Quality Forum or the LINC Health Panel, to work together in order to review and update the model for its continued use and durability.

2   Mechanisms should be put into place to ensure that library and information services are supported in their use of self-assessment techniques. Networks and contacts between those services undertaking self-assessment should be fostered, developed and supported.

3   Training programmes should be implemented by library and information services wishing to undertake self-assessment. Without an adequate understanding of the context or the process of self-assessment, the value of the approach will be dissipated.

4   Self-assessment should be used to support and sustain library and information service planning, improvement and development. Undertaken annually, it will provide a useful tool for understanding what the service is achieving.

5   Cross-sector benchmarking against the LISIM should be developed as a key tool for the continued improvement of library and information services.

6   The approach indicated by the LISIM should be integrated into the DCMS library planning procedures, and used by managers to support other planning frameworks adopted across the public library and information sector.

Public libraries have been a much loved public service for many years. New developments, such as the expansion of information and communication technologies, and the greater emphasis on accountability, present library and information sector managers with challenges and opportunities. The self-assessment approach described in this book is offered as a management tool to help public-service professionals and policy makers to demonstrate and maintain the public library as an essential public service.

References

Milner, E, Kinnell, M and Usherwood, B (1997) Quality management and public library services. In Brockman, J (ed) *Quality management and benchmarking in the information sector*, Bowker-Saur.

Reed, D (1997) *Public sector excellence research report*, British Quality Foundation.

Samuels, M (1998) *Towards best practice: an evaluation of the first two years of the public sector benchmarking project 1996-1998*, Cabinet Office Next Steps Team.

Whitford, B and Bird, R (1996) *The pursuit of quality: how organisations in the UK are attaining excellence through quality certification and total quality management systems*, Prentice Hall.

Winter, R (1996) Some principles and procedures for the conduct of action research. In Zuber-Skeritt, O *New directions in action research*, Falmer Press.

Wright, A (1997) Public service quality: lessons not learned, *Total Quality Management*, **8** (5), 313-20.

Bibliography

Alston, R (1995) Performance indicators in Bromley - purpose and practice, *Library Management*, **16** (1), 18-28.

Andersen, B and Pettersen P-G (1996) *The benchmarking handbook: step by step instructions*, Chapman & Hall.

Anonymous (1995) The straining of quality, *The Economist*, (14 January), 65.

Aslib (1995) *Review of the public library service in England and Wales for the Department of National Heritage: final report*, Aslib.

Audit Commission (1993) *Putting quality on the map*, Audit Commission.

Avery, C and Zabel, D (1997) *The quality management sourcebook: an international guide to materials and resources*, Routledge.

Bang, T, Clausen, H, Dyrskov, s E, Johannsen, C G and Johnsen, O (1996) *ISO9000 for library and information centres: a guide. Report of a project supported by NORDINFO*. FID Occasional Paper 13, FID.

Barnard, S B (1993) Implementing total quality management: a model for research libraries. In Jurow, S and Barnard, S B (eds) *Integrating total quality management in a library setting*, The Haworth Press.

Barratt, C, Slater, J and Morgan, D (1992) *Quality techniques: the quality management library*, HMSO.

Batt, C (1995) Pass the quality, please, *Library Manager*, **8**, 24.

Bigelow B, and Arndt M (1995) Total quality management: field of dreams?, *Health Care Management Review*, **20** (4), 15-25.

Black, S A and Porter, L J (1996) Identification of the critical factors of TQM, *Decision Sciences*, **27** (1), 1-21.

Black, S A and Crumbley, H C (1997) Self-assessment what's in it for us?, *Total Quality Management*, **8** (2/3), 90-3.

Boekhorst, P t (1995) Measuring quality: the IFLA guidelines for performance measurement in academic libraries, *IFLA Journal*, **21** (4), 278-81.

Boelke, J H (1995) *Quality improvement in libraries: total quality management and related approaches*. Advances in Librarianship 19, Academic Press.

Boland, T and Silbergh, D (1996) Managing for quality, *International Review of Administrative Sciences*, **62** (3), 351-67.

Borchardt, P (1999) Qualitätsmanagement in der Bibliothek umsetzen – wie geht das? Ergebnisse eines britischen Projekts, *Buch und Bibliothek*, **51**, 60-1.

Bossink, B A, Gieskes, J F B and Pas, T N M (1992) Diagnosing total quality management – part 1, *Total Quality Management*, **3** (3), 223-31.

Bossink, B A, Gieskes, J F B and Pas, T N M (1993) Diagnosing total quality management – part 2, *Total Quality Management*, **4** (1), 5-12.

BQF (1997) *Guide to self-assessment: public sector guidelines*, British Quality Foundation.

BQF (1998) *Quality links*, British Quality Foundation.

Brereton, M (1996) Introducing self-assessment – one of the keys to business excellence, *Management Services*, **40** (2), 22-3.

Brockman, J (1992) Just another management fad? The implications of TQM for library and information services, *Aslib Proceedings*, **44** (7/8), 283-8.

Brockman, J (1992) Test of total quality management (TQM) self-assessment guide at Woolwich and Bromley libraries, *Defence Librarian: Newsletter for MOD Librarians*, **23**, 16-17.

Brockman, J (1997) MoD locks on SMART, *UK Excellence*, (December), **14**, 16-17.

Brockman, J (ed) (1997) *Quality management and benchmarking in the information sector*, Bowker-Saur.

Brockman, J and Gilchrist, A (1995) Information management and the pursuit of corporate excellence, *FID News Bulletin*, **45** (5), 160-6.

Brophy, P and Coulling, K (1996) *Quality management for information and library managers*, Aslib Gower.

Brophy, P and Coulling, K (1997) Quality management in libraries. In Brockman, J (ed) *Quality management and benchmarking in the information sector*, Bowker-Saur.

Burton, C et al (1996) *London: library city. The public library service in London: a strategic review*, Comedia.

Byrne, D (1993) Quality management in library and information services, *The Law Librarian*, **24** (2), 69-74.

Cabinet Office (1999) New quality scheme taskforce announced. Press release (January), CAB 23/99.

Cabinet Office Service First Unit (1999) *How to improve your services: a guide to quality schemes for the public sector*, Cabinet Office.

Campbell, S J, Donelly, M and Wisniewski, M (1995) A measurement of service, *Scottish Libraries*, **50**, 10-11.

Carter, N et al (1992) *How organisations measure success: the use of performance indicators in government*, Routledge.

Carvell, J (1997) School results: shaming and acclaiming, *The Guardian G2*, (18 November), 2.

Catt, M E (1995) The Olympic training field for planning quality library services, *Library Trends*, **43** (3), 367-83.

Cave, M, Copley, G and Hanney, S (1995) Setting quality standards in the public sector: some principles and an application, *Public Money and Management*, (Jan-March), 29-34.

Clarke, M and Stewart, J (1990) *Developing effective public service management*, Local Government Training Board.

Clausen, H (1995) The Nordic Information Quality project: the final report, *New Library World*, **96** (1121), 4-10.

Clayton, C (1993) Quality and the public services, *Public Library Journal*, **8** (1), 11-12.

Conti, T (1997) Optimising self-assessment, *Total Quality Management*, **8** (2/3), 5-15.

Conti, T (1997) *Organisational self-assessment*, Chapman & Hall.

Couwenberg, C et al (1997) Assessing an organisation with the quality model, *European Management Journal*, **15** (3), 318-25.

Curtis, M (1993) Quality in Kent, *Public Library Journal*, **8** (1), 1-4.

Darrymple, J F and Donnelly M (1997) Managing and evaluating customer complaint procedures in local government, *Total Quality Management*, **8** (2/3) 130-4.

Davies, A and Kirkpatrick, I (1995) Face to face with the sovereign customer: service quality and the changing role of professional academic librarians, *Sociological Review*, 782-807.

Davison, J and Grieves, J (1996) Why should local government show an interest in service quality?, *TQM Magazine*, **8** (5), 32-8.

Dawes, S (1997) Managing with quality assurance, *Library Management*, **18** (2), 73-9.

DCMS (1997) *Annual library plan: guidelines*, Department of Culture, Media and Sport.

Dearing, R (1997) *Higher education in the learning society: report of the national committee*, HMSO.

Domas White, M and Abels, E G (1995) Measuring service quality in special libraries: lessons from service marketing, *Special Libraries*, **36** (1), 36-45.

DuPont, L R (1997) The criteria: a looking glass to Americans' understanding of quality, *Quality Progress*, **30** (9), 89-95.

Eastman, C J and Fulop L (1996) Total quality management: panacea or placebo for hospital management?, *International Journal of Public Administration*, **19** (11/12), 2141-66.

Easton, G (1995) A Baldrige examiner's assessment of US total quality management. In Cole, R E (ed) *The death and life of the American quality movement*, Oxford University Press.

Edge, J (1990) Quality improvement activities and techniques. In Lock, D (ed) *Gower handbook of quality management*, Gower.

EFQM (1997) *Guide to self-assessment 1997*, European Foundation for Quality Management.

Excellence Northwest (1997) *Self-assessment workbook and scoring table*, Excellence Northwest.

FEFC (1997) *Validating self-assessment*, Reference number 97/12, FEFC.

Foley, E G (1994) *Winning European quality*, European Foundation for Quality Management.

Frank, R C (1993) Total quality management: the Federal Government experience. In Jurow, S and Barnard, S B, (eds) *Integrating total quality management in a library setting*, The Haworth Press.

Freeman-Bell, G and Grover, R (1994) The use of quality management in local authorities, *Local Government Review*, **20** (4), 554-69.

Garavatta, M (1997) Conducting an organisational self-assessment using the 1997 Baldrige award criteria, *Quality Progress*, **30** (10), 87-91.

Garrod, P and Kinnell, M (1995) *Quality management issues: a select bibliography for library and information services managers,* British Library Research & Development Report 6220, FID Occasional Paper 20, FID.

Garrod, P and Kinnell, M (1997) Benchmarking development needs in the LIS sector, *Journal of Information Science,* **23** (2), 111-18.

Garrod, P and Kinnell, M (1997) Towards library excellence: best practice benchmarking in the library and information sector. In Brockman, J (ed) *Quality management and benchmarking in the information sector,* Bowker-Saur.

Gaster, L (1995) *Quality in public services,* Open University Press.

Ghobadian, A and Seng Woo, H (1996) Characteristics, benefits and shortcomings of four major quality awards, *International Journal of Quality and Reliability Management,* **13** (2),10-44.

Gilchrist, A and Brockman, J (1996) Where is the Xerox Corporation of the LIS sector?, *Library Trends,* **43** (3), 595-604.

Gillman, P (1992) Snares and delusions: the mis-management of quality. In *Total Quality Management: the information business: key issue 92,* University of Hertfordshire Press.

Goulding, A, Mistry, V, Proctor, R and Kinnell, M (1999) *Investing in LIS people: the impact of the IiP initiative on the library and information centre,* BLRIC. (Forthcoming)

Hackman, J R and Wageman, R (1995) Total quality management: empirical conceptual and practical issues, *Administrative Science Quarterly,* **40**, 309-42.

Hakes, C (1994) *Corporate self-assessment handbook,* Chapman & Hall.

Harvey, L and Green, D (1993) Defining quality, *Assessment & Evaluation in Higher Education,* **18** (1), 9-34.

Harwick, B T and Russell, M (1993) Quality criteria for public service: a working model, *International Journal of Service Industry Management,* **4** (2), 29-40.

Harwick, B T and Russell, M (1996) A working model to help institutionalise quality improvements in local government, *International Journal of Public Administration,* **19** (10), 1891-1913.

Hawkey, P (1993) Foot down on the quality drive, *Local Government Chronicle,* (30 April), 14.

Henderson, D (1992) *Report on the feasibility of a new UK quality award,* Department of Trade and Industry.

Henty, M (1989) Performance indicators in higher education libraries, *British Journal of Academic Librarianship*, **4** (13), 177-90.

Herget, J (1995) The cost of (non)quality: why it matters for information providers, *FID News Bulletin*, **45** (5), 156-9.

Hogget, P (1991) A new management in the public sector, *Policy and Politics*, **19** (4), 243-56.

Holloway, B (1995) Gaining the benefits of self-assessment, *Quality World*, (June), 404-6.

Holt, G E (1996) On becoming essential: an agenda for quality in twenty-first century public libraries, *Library Trends*, **44** (3), 545-71.

IFLA (1997) *National reports on performance measurement and quality management in public libraries. IFLA Satellite Meeting August 25-28, 1997,* Zentral- und Landsbibliothek Berlin - Stadtbüchereien, Düsseldorf - Deutsches Bibliothekinstitut.

Irving, A (1992) Quality in academic libraries how shall we know it?, *Aslib Information*, **20** (6), 244-6.

Johannsen, G C (1995) Application of quality management in the Nordic countries: results from the Nordic Quality Management Project, *FID News Bulletin*, **45** (5), 149-52.

Joint Funding Council's Library Review Group (1993) *Report*, Higher Education Funding Council for England.

Jones, K, Kinnell, M and Usherwood, B (1998) *Assessment tools for quality management in public libraries: report of the first project workshop*, Department of Information and Library Studies, Loughborough University.

Jones, K, Kinnell, M and Usherwood, B (1998) Self-assessment for quality management: a useful management tool or just management hype?, *Public Library Journal*, **13** (3), 33-7.

Jones, K, Kinnell, M and Usherwood, B (1998) The development of self-assessment tool-kits for the library and information sector, *Journal of Documentation*. (Forthcoming)

Jones, K, Kinnell, M and Usherwood, B (1999) *Planning for public library improvement: report of the second project workshop*, Department of Information and Library Studies, Loughborough University.

Jordan, P and Jones, N (1995) *Staff management in the library and information work*, 3rd edn, Gower.

Joss, R and Kogan, M (1995) *Advancing quality: total quality management in the National Health Service*, Open University Press.

Jurow, S (1993) Tools for measuring and improving performance. In Jurow, S and Barnard, S B (eds) *Integrating total quality management in a library setting*, The Haworth Press.

Jurow, S and Barnard, S B (eds) (1993) *Integrating total quality management in a library setting*, The Haworth Press.

Karlsson, S and Wiklund, P S (1997) Critical aspects of quality method implementation, *Total Quality Management*, **8** (1), 55-65.

Keiser, B E (1993) Quality management for libraries: a North American perspective, *Aslib Information*, **21** (6), 252-5.

Kerslake, E and Kinnell, M (1996) *Report to the British Library Research and Innovation Centre: quality management for library and information services policy forum*, Department of Information and Library Studies, Loughborough University.

Kinnell, M (1995) Quality management and library and information services: competitive advantage for the information revolution, *IFLA Journal*, **21** (4), 265-73.

Kinnell, M and MacDougall, J (1997) *Marketing in the not-for-profit sector*, Butterworth-Heinemann.

Kirkpatrick, I and Martinez Lucio, M (1995) *The politics of quality in the public sector: the management of change*, Routledge.

Kovel-Jarboe, P (1996) Quality improvement: a strategy for planned organisational change, *Library Trends*, **44** (3), 605-30.

Laree Jacques, M. (1996) 50 years of quality: an anniversary retrospective, *TQM Magazine*, 8 (4), 5-16.

Laszlo, G P (1995) Quality awards - recognition or model, *TQM Magazine*, **8** (5),14-18.

Lawes, A (1993) The benefits of quality management to the library and information services profession, *Special Libraries*, **84** (3), 142-6.

Lester, D (1994) The impact of quality management on the information sector: a study of case histories, EUSIDIC.

LGMB (1997) *Portrait of change*, Local Government Management Board.

LGMB (1997) *Quality initiatives: report of the findings from the 1997 of local authority activity*, Local Government Management Board.

Library and Information Commission (1997) *New library: the people's network*, Library and Information Commission.

LINC Health Panel (1997) *Accreditation of library and information services in the health sector: a checklist to support assessment*, LINC Health Panel Accreditation Working Group.

Linley, R and Usherwood, B (1998) *New measures for the new library: a social audit of public libraries*. British Library Research and Innovation Centre Report 89, Department of Information Studies, University of Sheffield.

Lloyds TSB (1996) *Quality in education: school self-assessment - how to make the business excellence model work for your school*, Lloyds TSB Group plc.

Loney, T J (1996) TQM and labour-management co-operation: a noble experiment for the public sector, *International Journal of Public Administration*, **19** (10), 1845-63.

McIntyre, B (1994) Measuring excellence in public libraries, *Australian Public Libraries and Information Services*, **7** (3), 135-55.

McKevitt, D and Lawton, A (1996) The manager, the citizen, the politician and performance measures, *Public Money and Management*, **16** (3), 49-54.

Mackey, T and Mackey, K (1992) Think quality! The Deming approach does work in libraries, *Library Journal*, (15 May), 57-61.

Madsen, O N (1995) Public enterprise and total quality management, *Total Quality Management*, **6** (2), 165-73.

Marsh, J (1993) *The quality tool-kit: an A-Z of tools and techniques*, IFS International.

Massey, A (1993) *Managing the public sector. a comparative analysis of the UK and US*, Edward Elgar.

Matarasso, F (1998) *Beyond book issues: the social potential of library projects*, Comedia.

Maxwell, R J (1984) Quality assessment in health, *British Medical Journal*, **288**, 1470-1.

Mendelsohn, S (1995) Can you cost quality?, *Library Manager*, **4**, 6, 8-9.

Mendelsohn, S (1995) Does your library come up to scratch?, *Library Manager*, **8**, 6, 8-9.

Miller, R G and Stearns, B (1994) Quality management for today's academic library, *College and Research Libraries News*, **48**, 110-22.

Milner, E, Kinnell, M and Usherwood, B (1994) Quality management: the public library debate, *Public Library Journal*, **9** (6), 151-7.

Milner, E, Kinnell, M and Usherwood, B (1995) Employee suggestion schemes: a management tool for the 1990s, *Library Management*, **16** (3), 3-8.

Milner, E, Kinnell, M and Usherwood, B, (1997). Quality management and public library services. In Brockman, J (ed) *Quality management and benchmarking in the information sector*, Bowker-Saur.

Morgan, C and Murgatroyd, S (1994) *TQM in the public sector: an international perspective*, Open University Press.

Morgan, S (1995) Customer orientation: more than a passing phase?, *Library Manager*, **3**, 20-1.

Morgan, S (1995) *Performance assessment in academic libraries*, Mansell.

Mullen, J A (1993) Total quality management: a mindset and method to stimulate change, *Journal of Library Administration*, **18** (3/4), 91-108.

Oldroyd, M (ed) (1996) *Staff development in academic libraries: present practice and future challenges*, Library Association Publishing.

Owlia, M S and Aspinall, E S (1997) TQM in higher education - a review, *International Journal of Quality and Reliability Management*, **14** (5), 527-43.

Pfeffer, N and Coote, A (1991) *Is quality good for you?*, Institute of Public Policy Research.

Poister, T H and Henry, G T (1994) Citizen rating of public and private service quality: a comparative perspective, *Public Administration Review*, **54** (2), 155-60.

Pollalis, Y A (1996) A systemic approach to change management: integrating information systems planning, BPR and TQM, *Information Systems Management*, **13** (2), 19-25.

Pollit, C (1990) Doing business in the temple? Managers and quality assurance in the public services, *Public Administration*, **68**, 435-52.

Pollit, C (1993) The struggle for quality - the case of the National Health Service, *Policy and Politics*, **21** (3), 161-70.

Porter, L (1992) Quality Assurance: going round in circles, *Aslib Information*, **20** (6) 40-241.

Porter, L (1993) *Quality initiatives in British library and information services*. British Library Research and Innovation Centre Report 6105, BLRIC.

Porter, L J and Parker, A J (1993) Total quality management - the critical success factors, *Total Quality Management*, **4** (1), 1993.

Pritchard, S M (1996) Determining quality in academic libraries, *Library Trend*, **44** (3), 572-94.

Public Management Foundation (1997) *Hitting local targets: the public value of public services*, Public Management Foundation.

Quinn, B (1997) Adapting service quality concepts to academic libraries, *The Journal of Academic Librarianship*, (September), 359-69.

Redman, T (1995) Quality management in services: is the public sector keeping pace?, *International Journal of Public Sector Management*, 21-34.

Reed, D (1995) Public test on the award model, *UK Quality*, (September), 10-11.

Reed, D (1997) *Public sector excellence research report*, British Quality Foundation.

Rowley, J (1996) Managing quality in information services, *Information Services & Use*, **16** (1), 51-61.

Rowley, J (1996) Implementing TQM for library services: the issues, *Aslib Proceedings*, **48** (1), 17-18, 21.

St Clair, G (1994) *Power and influence: enhancing information services within the organisation*, Bowker-Saur.

St Clair, G (1996) TQM: the battle isn't won yet, *Library Manager*, **17**, 14-15.

Samuels, M (1998) *Towards best practice: an evaluation of the first two years of the public sector benchmarking project 1996-1998*, Cabinet Office Next Steps Team.

Sanderson, I (ed) (1992) *Management of quality in local government*, Longman.

SCONUL (1992) *Performance Indicators for university libraries: a practical guide*, SCONUL.

Seay, T, Seaman, S and Cohen, D (1996) Measuring and improving the quality of public services: a hybrid approach, *Library Trends*, **44** (3), 464-90.

Shaughnessy, T W (1996) Perspectives on quality in libraries, *Library Trends*, **44** (3), 459-678.

Shergold, K and Reed, D (1996) Striving for excellence: how self-assessment using the Business Excellence Model can result in step improvements in all areas of business activities, *TQM Magazine*, **8** (6), 48-52.

Sirkin, A F (1993) Customer service: another side of TQM. In Jurow, S and Barnard, S B (eds) *Integrating total quality management in a library setting*, The Haworth Press.

Smith, P (1993) Outcome related performance indicators and organisational control in the public sector, *British Journal of Management*, **4**, 135-51.

Society of Information Management working groups on quality (1992) *Quality assessment and planning tools for IS for specifying the elements and levels of information systems quality*, Society of Information Management.

Spiller, D (ed) (1998) *Public library plans. Proceedings of a seminar held at Loughborough University 17 -18 March 1998*, LISU.

Stewart, J and Walsh, K (1989) *The search for quality*, Local Government Training Board.

Stewart, J and Walsh, K (1992) Change in the management of public services, *Public Administration*, **70**, 499-518.

Swedish National Council for Cultural Affairs (1995) *Evaluating the GOK project: the innovative capacity of the Swedish library system*, Statens Kulturrad.

Talbot, C (1998) *Public performance: towards a public service excellence model. Discussion paper* (personal communication).

TQMI (1995) *What is self assessment?*, TQM International.

TQMI (1997) *Managing a self-assessment process*, TQM International.

Tyerman, K (1996) Getting things in focus: the use of focus groups in Brent Libraries, *Library Management*, **17** (2), 36-9.

Usherwood, B (1992) Managing public libraries as a public service, *Public Library Journal*, **7** (6), 141-5.

Usherwood, B (1996) *Rediscovering public library management*, Library Association Publishing.

Usherwood, B (1998) Much more than numbers, *The Bookseller*, (8 May), 28-9.

Van der Wiele, T et al (1995) A study of progress in Europe's leading organisations in quality management practices, *International Journal of Quality and Reliability Management*, **13** (1), 84-104.

Van Der Wiele, T et al (1995) State of the art study on self-assessment, *TQM Magazine*, 7 (4), 13-15.

Van Der Wiele, T et al (1996) Quality management self-assessment: an examination in European business, *Journal of General Management*, 22 (1), 48-67.

Walsh, K (1991) Quality and public services, *Public Administration*, **69**, 503-14.

Walsh, K (1995) Quality through markets: the new public service management. In Wilkinson, A and Willmott, H (eds) *Making quality critical: new perspectives on organisational change*, International Thomson Business Press.

Ward, J A (1996) Measurement management: what you measure is what you get, *Information Systems Management*, **13** (1), 59-61.

Ward, S, Sumsion, J, Fuegi, D and Bloar, I (1995) *Library performance indicators and library management models*, European Commission.

Whitehall, T (1992) Quality in library and information services: a review, *Library Management*, **13** (5), 23-35.

Whitford, B and Bird, R (1996) *The pursuit of quality: how organisations in the UK are attaining excellence through quality certification and total quality management systems*, Prentice Hall.

Weingand, D E (1997) *Customer service excellence: a concise guide for librarians*, American Library Association.

Wilding, P (1994) Maintaining quality in human services, *Social Policy & Administration*, **28** (1), 57-72.

Wilkinson, A and Willmott, H (eds) (1995) *Making quality critical: new perspectives on organisational change*, International Thomson Business Press.

Wilkinson, A and Willmott, H (1996) Quality management, problems and pitfalls: a critical perspective, *International Journal of Quality and Reliability Management*, **13** (2), 55-65.

Wilkinson, A, Redman, T and Snape, E (1993) *Quality and the manager: an IM report*, Institute of Management.

Williamson, V and Exon, F C A (1996) The quality movement in Australian University Libraries, *Library Trends*, **44** (3), 526-44.

Winter, R (1996) Some principles and procedures for the conduct of action research. In Zuber-Skeritt, O *New directions in action research*, Falmer Press.

Wressel, P (ed) (1995) *Proceedings of the 1st Northumbria International Conference on Performance Measurement in libraries and information services, 31 August-4 September 1995*, Information North.

Wright, A (1997) Public service quality: lessons not learned, *Total Quality Management*, **8** (5), 313-20.

Zaremba, D and Crew, T (1997) Increasing involvement in self-assessment: the Royal Mail approach, *The TQM Magazine*, **7** (2), 29-32.

Index

Developing Information and Library Staff through Work-based Learning
101 activities

BARBARA ALLAN

In times of financial constraint, an organization's staff development budget is often the first to be reduced. This can have disastrous consequences in a period when rapid technological and other changes require library and information workers to constantly update their knowledge and skills.

This practical book aims to provide the solution to this problem. Packed with helpful advice and practical tips, it describes a resourceful, alternative approach to staff development based on work-based learning methods, self-development and in-house resources, which offers a means of focusing learning on the needs of the individual.

The book is organized into three parts. Part One introduces practical strategies for the development and management of learning skills in the workplace, including:

- a rationale for developing work-based learning
- individual learning in the workplace
- developing independence in learning in the workplace
- developing work-based learning
- developing a learning organization.

Part Two comprises 101 methods of work-based learning in library and information organizations. Organized alphabetically, these cover techniques as diverse as secondments, learning contracts, project work, job-rotation, teamwork, feedback, cross-sectoral working, mentoring, mind-mapping and many more. The author describes each method's application in detail, often with a practical workplace example of its implementation.

Part Three is a useful guide to resources currently available on work-based learning.

Written in an easy-to-read, accessible style, this innovative text is an essential companion for library and information managers, supervisors, personnel officers and trainers in all sectors, and for any information staff wishing to maintain a skilled workforce in the face of training budget cuts.

1999; 208pp; hardback; 1-85604-281-2; £29.95

Managing Library Services for Children and Young People
a practical handbook

Catherine Blanshard

In the light of the current financial climate of cutbacks and competing priorities, it is becoming increasingly important to review children's and youth services in order to make them relevant and marketable to their audience, and to attract funding and sponsorship for the service.

This practical handbook shows how library managers can make use of ideas taken from current business practice to evaluate and assess the library service, and how this can result in value and quality being added to the services offered.

This text answers a real need for a hands-on manual for the practitioner in this sector. Emphasizing that the needs of the child and of the young person should drive management decisions, it demonstrates how these can best be addressed by the implementation of service specifications, business plans, targets, profiles and strategies.

Dealing with such diverse areas as: finding out what children want, display and promotion, measuring quality, and providing a young peoples' information strategy, this accessible handbook provides service managers with a manual of best practice within each area of the service, including:

- managing change
- the users of children's libraries
- managing the children's service
- managing performance
- strategic management
- key service issues
- stock related issues.

This book is essential reading for service managers in public libraries, senior managers in local government, school librarians, governors and teachers and all those concerned with the provision of library services to children and young people.

1998; 208pp hardback; 1-85604-226-X; £37.50

Becoming a Successful Intrapreneur
A Practical Guide to Creating an Innovative Information Service

SHEILA PANTRY AND PETER GRIFFITHS

Information services of all kinds need to be proactive within their institution by using entrepreneurial skills internally, marketing themselves vigorously and emphasizing their value to other departments and sections. This book offers the LIS professional a systematic approach to ways of demonstrating the service's worth and achieving wide support within the organization. It also aims to promote a new intrapreneurial style of information skills to meet the challenges of a rapidly changing information landscape, including: intelligence gathering, squaring up to knowledge management, developing vision, taking risks, turning information into a value-added service, and using performance measures.

Using cross-sectoral case studies, examples, worksheets and summaries the book offers guidance on:

- strategic approaches to intrapreneurship
- pursuing the aims and objectives of your organization
- conducting an internal information audit
- keeping one step ahead of the customer
- offering and delivering innovative services
- building the perfect team
- setting and maintaining standards
- marketing and promotion.

This book is essential reading for those LIS managers and professionals who wish to maximize the benefit of using new skills to provide truly customer-oriented and innovative information services.

1998; 112pp; paperback; 1-85604-292-8; £13.50